The First Lady of Olympic Track

# The
# First Lady
# of Olympic
# Track

## THE LIFE AND TIMES OF BETTY ROBINSON

Joe Gergen

NORTHWESTERN UNIVERSITY PRESS
EVANSTON, ILLINOIS

Northwestern University Press
www.nupress.northwestern.edu

Printed in the United States of America

10  9  8  7  6  5  4  3  2  1

**Library of Congress Cataloging-in-Publication Data**

Gergen, Joe, author.
    The first lady of Olympic track : the life and times of Betty Robinson /
      Joe Gergen.
      pages cm
    Includes bibliographical references and index.
    ISBN 978-0-8101-2958-0 (pbk. : alk. paper)
      1. Robinson, Betty, 1911–1999. 2. Runners (Sports)—United States—
Biography. 3. Women Olympic athletes—United States—Biography.
4. Women runners—United States—Biography. I. Title.
GV1061.15.R62G47 2014
796.42092—dc23

                              2013035620

*For*

*Rick Schwartz and Jane Schwartz Hamilton,*

*who inherited the torch,*

*and for*

*Brook Hamilton Doire and Marie Gergen Cuevas,*

*whose friendship provided the inspiration*

For in all things there is but one first.
And for all time Betty Robinson will be
remembered as the first gold medal winner
in the history of women's track and field.

—BUD GREENSPAN,
Olympic filmmaker and historian,
in the documentary
*America's Greatest Olympians*

# CONTENTS

Introduction                                                3

CHAPTER 1    Riverdale                                      9

CHAPTER 2    Amelia Earhart Sailed Here                    19

CHAPTER 3    Soft Landing                                  29

CHAPTER 4    Golden Girl                                   39

CHAPTER 5    Fit for a Queen                               47

CHAPTER 6    New York                                      57

CHAPTER 7    Parade Rest                                   63

CHAPTER 8    Sexual Politics                               69

CHAPTER 9    Senior Moment                                 77

CHAPTER 10   Crash                                         85

CHAPTER 11   Down and Out                                  95

CHAPTER 12   Heil Brundage!                               105

CHAPTER 13   Last Voyage                                  115

CHAPTER 14   Torch Song                                   125

CHAPTER 15   Power Play                        133

CHAPTER 16   Third Reich, Third Medal          141

CHAPTER 17   (Nazi) Party Time                 149

CHAPTER 18   Love and Marriages               159

CHAPTER 19   Home Stretch                      167

CHAPTER 20   Legacy                            173

             Notes                             177

             Index                             185

*Photographs follow page 94.*

The First Lady of Olympic Track

# Introduction

At the far end of the gangplank, welcoming U.S. Olympians aboard the SS *President Roosevelt* bound for the 1928 Summer Games in Amsterdam, stood the general. To Betty Robinson and her eighteen peers on the women's track and field team, the presence of Douglas MacArthur was both a measure of how far they had come and a symbol of the challenge that lay ahead. With their next few steps, they would be embarking on a great adventure not just for themselves but for millions of female Americans.

Women in the United States had gained the right and responsibility to vote only eight years earlier. Just the previous month Amelia Earhart had become the first woman to cross the Atlantic Ocean in a flying machine, a feat that inspired a ticker-tape parade in New York even though she was merely along for the ride. (This was four years before her legendary solo transatlantic flight.) In a decade of unprecedented advancement for the so-called fair sex, the perception was that Robinson and her teammates were confronting another barrier, competing in the first Olympics to allow women in the traditional sports of track and field.

Opposition had been fierce. Baron Pierre de Coubertin, founder of the modern Olympics in 1896, was among their foremost adversaries. The French aristocrat patterned his Games after those staged by the ancient Greeks, which excluded women from the competition. "The Olympic Games are the solemn and periodic exaltation of male athleticism," he wrote in 1912, "with internationalism as a base, loyalty as a means, arts for its setting and female applause as reward."[1]

From the beginning, however, women athletes were not content with cheering on their male counterparts. They made slight inroads in 1900, participating in the ladylike sports of tennis and golf; provided a small group of archers for the 1904 edition in St. Louis; gained admission to select swimming events starting in 1912 at Stockholm; and joined the fencing competition at Paris in 1924. But they wanted more. They wanted equal access, especially to the events of greatest importance to the mythic residents of Olympia, the sweat-stained tests of speed and endurance that formed the core of the Games.

They had been denied for the better part of a decade despite the establishment of the National Women's Track and Field Committee under the chairmanship of Dr. Harry Eaton Stewart. A physician who encouraged competition for females and conducted studies on the effect of vigorous exercise on their hearts and blood pressure, he published papers that refuted the unscientific conclusions of many doctors and physical educators that athletics would impair women's child-bearing ability and shorten their lives. He also provided extensive information on equipment, training, and coaching methods.

While Stewart's committee was staging events and acting as a clearinghouse for records in the United States, a more ambitious project was under way in France, where Femina Sport, a club founded in 1911, sponsored the first national track and field championship for women in 1917. Among the members of that club was Alice Milliat, a translator by trade and a rowing enthusiast who was so committed to the cause that she was elected treasurer of the first national sports organization, the Fédération des Sociétés Féminines Sportives de France. Within fifteen months she had risen to general secretary and then president and petitioned the International

Olympic Committee to include women's track and field in the first postwar Games at Antwerp in 1920.

"After being turned down because track and field was deemed inappropriate competition for women," wrote journalist Kathleen McElroy, "[Milliat] founded the Fédération Sportive Féminine Internationale [FSFI], which created venues for women to compete outside of the IOC jurisdiction. In 1921, the Sporting Club of Monte Carlo staged the first international event for women. Certain that the success of this international meet would ensure sanctioning from the IOC, Milliat applied again. After another rejection from the 1924 Paris Games, the FSFI organized its own Women's Olympic Games in Paris in 1922 with sixty-five women from five countries competing in eleven events with twenty thousand spectators."[2]

The U.S. team, consisting of thirteen athletes, was assembled by Dr. Stewart. Not only did he convince the Amateur Athletic Union to authorize a team but he served as head coach and subsequently was elected vice president of the FSFI. The Americans finished second to the British and received mostly positive press coverage.

"The girls have become athletes," AAU president William Prout told the *New York Herald*. "We can't stop them. We must simply standardize their games."[3]

Although the one-day meet in Paris was a success by many standards, the IOC's immediate reaction was to demand the FSFI desist using the word "Olympic" in future promotions. But it also urged the International Amateur Athletic Federation (IAAF), which governed worldwide track and field, to negotiate with the women's federation and seek control of their events. The FSFI continued to sponsor its own "Olympics" in 1926 at Gothenburg, Sweden, but it adopted the title of International Ladies Games after the IAAF tentatively accepted a proposal for a full program of events for women's track and field in the 1928 Olympics at Amsterdam.

Such a progressive step, it should be noted, occurred only after de Coubertin resigned as president of the IOC in 1925. To have opposed his wishes while he was still in office would have been an insult and perhaps folly. "As to the admission of women to the Games," he said in 1928, "I remain strongly against it. It was against my will that they were admitted to a growing number of competitions."[4]

Even in his absence, there was so much dissension within the IOC membership that "only a watered down version of the original program was accepted. The Congress decided that five events would be admitted but only as 'an experiment.'"[5] While the FSFI voted grudgingly for the compromise, the British women's federation did not. It chose to boycott the competition.

Legislative issues aside, many critics clung to the moral argument that women athletes should be neither seen nor heard. A girls' gymnastics meet in Rome in the spring of 1928 earned a rebuke from Pope Pius XI. "After twenty centuries of Christianity," he wrote in one of several open letters critical of female performers leading up to the Olympics, "the sensitiveness and attention to the delicate care due young women and girls should be shown to have fallen lower than pagan Rome."[6]

It so happened that at the same meeting at which the IOC approved five trial events for women in track and field, it also authorized one event—the team combined exercises—for female gymnasts. And the Italian competitors were among the favorites.

The Pontiff's views were in line with the mores of the era. "If ever a woman must raise a hand, we hope and pray she may do so only in prayer or for acts of charity," he preached. "Everything must be avoided which contrasts with reserve and modesty, which are the ornament and safeguard of virtue."[7]

Against such a backdrop, ninety-five women from as far away as Japan and Australia prepared for competition in Amsterdam. The nineteen Americans ranged in age from high jumper Mildred Wiley, 26, to sprinter Olive Hasenfus, who was 15. At 16 years old, Robinson was among the youngest and least experienced. The Olympics would be her fourth official competition in a career which had begun months earlier.

The ship on which she was about to embark was the biggest she had ever seen in her life. It was large enough to house half the population of Riverdale, Illinois, the Cook County village where she was born and raised. Before the trip to Newark, New Jersey, for the Olympic trials the previous week, the farthest she had strayed from home was Stone Lake, in northern Indiana, where her family rented a cabin during the summer. Now, having just completed her junior year of high school, she was bound for Europe on an ocean liner with such established Olympic stars as Johnny Weissmuller, Bud Houser, and Charley Paddock under the direction of the youngest major general in the history of the United States.

MacArthur, a hero of the Great War, was on leave from the army when he was selected as president of the American Olympic Committee. Officials wanted someone who could heal the rifts between athletic organizations, instill discipline in the ranks, and command the allegiance of the strongest possible U.S. team in what was expected to be the most competitive Olympics to date. He fit the bill on all accounts and, even attired in civilian clothes, he projected military bearing in the smallest of encounters. The prospect of the ship, the trip, and the skip was cause for excitement among all those who streamed aboard the *President Roosevelt* at Pier 86 in New York on the morning of July 11. For the pioneer female class of 1928, the historic significance added to the sense of occasion, one that fairly buckled the knees.

---

# Riverdale

From the elevated platform in Harvey, Illinois, Charles Price could look back up Broadway toward Thornton Township High School, where he taught biology. On that weekday afternoon in the late winter of 1928, he could see several of his students walking in small groups toward the station and one, in particular, racing in his direction. As the Illinois Central commuter train pulled in and he stepped aboard, the man thought it was unfortunate that Betty Robinson had just missed her ride home.

Price did a double take a few seconds later when the junior sat down alongside him. He told her she must be very fast to have run up the stairs before the doors closed. A former track athlete in college, he was curious enough to ask her to don her gym clothes and tennis shoes the following day after school and sprint 50 yards down a school corridor.

She could always run fast, she explained, and had won a lot of ribbons at church and lodge picnics. But she had never been timed and didn't know there were organized races for girls, which was understandable because the Illinois State Athletic Association prohibited interscholastic competition for female track and field athletes.

"I had no idea that women even ran then," Robinson recalled

many years later. "That is when I found out that they actually had track meets for women."[1]

When Price checked the stopwatch held by senior Bob Williams the next afternoon, he suggested Robinson start training with the boys' team, and he said he would find her a meet in which to test herself against quality sprinters. After checking the newspapers, he pinpointed the American Institute of Banking Meet, an annual amateur competition scheduled at the Chicago Riding Club, an amphitheater near the lakefront that also hosted horse shows. Williams accompanied Robinson into the city, where she signed an entry form and purchased her first pair of track shoes.

Unknown to Robinson, her first race would be against one of the foremost athletes in the country. Helen Filkey was 20 years old and a star of the sport. She had won the Amateur Athletic Union championship in the 60-yard hurdles in each of the previous three years and held world records in the 100- and 70-yard dashes at different times in her career. And she didn't disappoint anyone in the capacity crowd that attended the bankers' meet on the night of March 30, 1928. The bold headline atop the March 31 edition of the *Chicago Tribune* noted that Filkey had shaved two-fifths of a second off the world indoor record for the hurdles, equaling her own outdoor mark. In a remarkable double, Filkey also tied the world indoor record for the 60-yard dash.

Nowhere in the story was mentioned the effort by Robinson in the first sanctioned race of her life. But under the results, in agate type, the inexperienced 16-year-old was listed second in the dash, and the Illinois Women's Athletic Club, which sponsored Filkey and other outstanding area competitors, took notice. Robinson was accorded an invitation to join the prestigious club and she accepted.

Chicago was in the throes of a building boom during the 1920s, and membership in the IWAC gave Robinson the chance to explore the wonders of the burgeoning metropolis. Her practice schedule required three train trips a week from her high school to the Randolph Street station in the Loop. From there she would take a bus or walk across the graceful bridge spanning the Chicago River, pass between the alabaster façade of the Wrigley Building, completed in 1924, and the neo-Gothic Tribune Tower, dedicated the following year, and make her way up North Michigan Avenue through an area that later would be designated the Magnificent Mile. The "City of the Big Shoulders," as Carl Sandburg had characterized Chicago in his 1916 poem, was flexing its muscles and pushing skyward.

The handsome redbrick headquarters of the IWAC had opened its doors just behind the iconic Water Tower in 1927. A social and residential club as well as a sports powerhouse, its athletic facilities occupied floors 14 through 16 of the skyscraper. "Because the building lacked an adequate indoor track, its teams trained in the nearby National Guard Armory during indoor seasons, and the rest of the year they practiced at adjacent Lake Shore playground."[2]

For the most part, the club's athletic endeavors remained separate from its social activities. The athletes were required to check in at the club, get their uniforms, walk to practice, then return to shower. Practices normally ran from midafternoon to well into evening in summer. The club had no coaching staff, per se, but coaches from DePaul University would help whenever the two squads shared practice space.

It made for a long school day for Robinson, whose home in the village of Riverdale was two stops north on the commuter train from her high school in Harvey. "I did a lot of traveling back and forth," she said. "I would go downtown, after school, and get there around four o'clock and wouldn't get home until seven or eight by the time I got to the track and worked out and got dressed again and took a bus back to the train to go home again. I really had a long trip. But it was worth it because I enjoyed it."[3]

Any doubt about the value of the regimen was erased in Robinson's first public appearance as a member of the IWAC on June 2, 1928. The setting was the Central AAU meet at massive Soldier Field, itself a recent addition to the Chicago scene and the host of the famous "long-count" match between Jack Dempsey and Gene Tunney for the world heavyweight championship the previous year. Because the meet was sponsored by the *Chicago Evening American,* it received an inordinate amount of attention in the Hearst paper noted for its aggressive and personalized journalism.

"Once upon a time if a woman did so much as run for a street-car, the natives stood by and gasped," Jimmy Corcoran, an *Evening American* reporter, wrote in advance of the meet. "You see, it wasn't supposed to be the proper thing to do, in as much as the constitution of the species, they said, couldn't stand exertion. Well, that was years ago. It was before the time that a girl discovered, probably much to her surprise, that she could run 50 yards without calling a doctor."[4]

Despite the paper's best attempts to conjure a crowd, including offering free admission, the event drew fewer spectators than those at the nearby Coliseum, where 137 couples were taking their first steps in a marathon dance contest for a purse of $3,500. But it trumpeted the arrival of a genuine star in Robinson, who, buffeted by a whistling north wind that coursed through the open end of the stadium, was timed in 12 seconds flat in both the semifinal and final heats of the 100-meter dash. That was four-tenths of a second better than the sanctioned world record and two-tenths of a second faster than any female reportedly had run the distance.

Although Robinson's time was not ratified by the FSFI because the wind was above the acceptable level, Robinson did succeed in beating Filkey by several strides and becoming an overnight sensation in Chicago. She explained:

> I just started in, pounding along and doing the best I could. When I saw that I was beating Helen, I knew I was going to win and eased up a bit. Suddenly I remembered they expected me to make some kind of record. Then I speeded up a bit.
>
> And then it was all over and I was standing there in dad's arms and he was hugging me so hard I thought he was going to crush all the breath out of me and telling me over and over again how proud of me he was.[5]

In an era when competing papers were not reluctant to own the news, the *Evening American* announced it would sponsor Robin-son's trip to the Olympic trials scheduled for the following month in Newark, New Jersey.

Her performance was well received in Robinson's hometown, particularly at 3 East 138th Street, where her family occupied all three floors of a traditional Chicago three-flat. Betty lived with her parents, Harry and Elizabeth (Wilson) Robinson, on the second floor while her oldest sister, Jean Rochfort, occupied the top floor with her husband and infant son, and another sister, Evelyn Mills, shared the first floor with her husband and two daughters (a son would arrive the following year). Since she was the youngest of her siblings by ten years, Betty was known throughout the house as the baby of the family or, simply, Babe.

As was the case with Chicago, Riverdale had experienced a sudden growth spurt due in part to the railroads that crisscrossed the community and provided, in addition to a sensory overload of steam and whistles, a healthy job market for the many blue-collar families in the area. In addition to the massive rail yard that served freight trains at the western end of town, Acme Steel relocated its plant to an area adjacent to the Calumet River in 1918 and the Federal Ice Refrigeration Company opened in 1919. The main line of the Illinois Central, which ferried passengers all the way south to New Orleans—as well as the newly electrified commuter train which carried her to and from school four miles away—was located two blocks from Robinson's house.

An A student, Robinson participated in music and theater at Thornton. But her first love was dance and she was not shy about performing, no matter how small the stage. Thomas Kinney, a childhood friend, recalled recruiting Betty for a tent show produced by neighborhood children in an empty field across from his house. "She had just finished her freshman year at Thornton," Kinney reported. "We did not know what to do about music to accompany her. She suggested 'Sweet Georgia Brown.'"

So the children spun a recording of the music on a borrowed Victrola and Robinson danced the Charleston to one of the more popular songs of the day. "She had to do two or three encores," Kinney recalled.[6]

Two summers later, she was off on a grand adventure, with little time for such diversions. Her training regimen grew more intense, and she had barely finished her final exams at Thornton before she, Filkey, and Nellie Todd, representing the IWAC, traveled to Union Station for the overnight train to Newark in the company of Mrs. Elizabeth Waterman, the club's athletic director, and Robinson's mother. The site was chosen for several reasons, not the least its proximity to New York, where the chartered ship for Amsterdam and the Olympic Games was scheduled to depart on July 11. Newark also held a prominent place in the brief history of women's track, since the New Jersey city hosted the initial national AAU championship in 1923, and the Prudential Insurance Company Athletic Association, founded in Newark, earned the first two team titles.

Of the three Chicago athletes who arrived in Newark on the morning of July 1, the inexperienced Robinson was accorded the best chance to succeed, because there was no hurdles event on the Olympic program. To qualify for the team, Filkey, regarded as the best in the world at her specialty, would have to earn a place in the 100 meters or in the 4 × 100-meter relay. Todd held the world broad jump record, but that event also was not featured in Amsterdam, so she entered the 800 meters without a previous race at a distance so unfamiliar to American women.

Robinson's East Coast profile received an unexpected boost thanks to her friends at the *Evening American,* who purchased a half-page ad in the Newark *Evening News* on the eve of the July 4 meet.

"The Chicago Evening American," it stated in bold letters, "wishes Elizabeth Robinson (the Chicago Evening American champion running in the colors of the Illinois Women's Athletic Club) all the luck in the world in her attempt to defeat all contestants in the Olympic trials for the 100-meter run."

Despite such unprecedented publicity, her appearance was overshadowed by the presence of the Northern California Athletic Club, which had easily won the team competition in the 1927 AAU championship at its home field in Eureka and brought the largest contingent to New Jersey despite the long train trip from the West Coast. The team was favored to dominate what the *Evening News,* in its gushing advance story, called "the greatest feminine track and field meet in the history of athletics."

Elta Cartwright, a 20-year-old student at Humboldt State Teachers College, was the standout of the Northern California team. The fourth of five daughters, she had been competing since elementary school and won her first national championship, in the 50-yard dash, in 1925 at the age of 17. She also finished second to Filkey in the 100. Cartwright repeated in the 50 in 1926 and again in 1927 and added the 100-yard title in 1927. In addition to her burgeoning reputation, she acquired a catchy nickname for her domination on the cinder tracks: Cinder-Elta.[7]

Robinson, Filkey, and Todd spent the night before the meet watching the races at the Newark Velodrome, which had hosted the first world cycling championships in 1912 and remained among the most popular venues for the sport. By the time they reported to Newark Schools Stadium—a concrete horseshoe that boasted a capacity of 15,000—the following afternoon, the temperature was pushing a season-high 90 degrees and residents were heading to the beaches on the Jersey Shore for relief. Only an estimated 1,500 spectators, approximately six for each of the 250 participants, gathered under the broiling sun.

Not surprisingly, the lone sprint race drew the largest field and the greatest interest. Of the eight preliminary heats, Cartwright, Robinson, and Filkey were winners—along with Jessie Cross, Loretta McNeil, and Mary Washburn, all from the Millrose Athletic Association in New York; Anne Vrana of the Pasadena (California) AC; and Olive Hasenfus, representing the Boston Swimming Association. Filkey, considered the best female athlete in the country three years earlier when she won three events at the AAU championships, tripped in the first semifinal heat while Cross and Edna Sayer of Brooklyn advanced to the final. Filkey would go on to win the 60-yard hurdles for a fourth consecutive year, but that was small consolation for her failure in the only event that could earn her passage to Amsterdam.

Vrana and Robinson won the second and third semifinal heats before Cartwright easily triumphed in the fourth, equaling the best time of the meet (12.4) set by Cross in the first heat. The final that followed not only tested the ladies' speed but also their endurance. It marked the first time Robinson had to race three times in competition. She was assigned the second lane in the final while Cartwright started from the far outside in lane eight.

The two quickly turned the dash into a match race, but the experienced Cartwright had the advantage of a better start and Robinson never could make up the difference. The Riverdale teenager had to take solace in finishing a clear second and extending Cartwright to the limit. Not that it appeared to have an immediate impact on the winner. She went from that event to dominate the 50-yard dash.

"My coach, Laura Herron, said it would be wonderful to get a third gold medal," Cartwright recalled in an interview with her hometown newspaper decades later. "So I said, 'I'm going to do it.' I just made up my mind and jumped out there and got my third medal."[8] That was in the broad jump, where she leaped 16 feet, 10¾ inches to defeat local girl Elizabeth Grobes by more than five inches. In all, Cinder-Elta scored more points than all but one other team, the Pasadena AC, and led Northern California's defense of its championship.

Nellie Todd was not a factor in the 800, won by Rayma Wilson from Pasadena on the basis of the best time in three heats before a severe thunderstorm, accompanied by high winds, swept across the track. "Everyone who was in the later events like me was drenched," said Margaret Jenkins, a teammate of Cartwright who won the javelin toss but qualified for the Olympic team with her third-place finish in the discus.[9]

At the end of the competition, AAU officials chose nineteen individuals to represent the United States in the Olympic Games. There were eight sprinters, four for the 100 meters—Cartwright, Robinson, Vrana, and Washburn—and the other four—Cross, Hasenfus, McNeil, and Sayer—were selected as alternates and potential relay members. At the age of 15 years, 9 months, Hasenfus was the youngest track and field participant. High jumper Jean Shiley was 16 years and 8 months, followed by Robinson and Vrana, both 16 years, 11 months. Vrana was one day older than Robinson.

Before she left Newark for New York and the next step of her improbable journey, Robinson drafted a letter to her sponsors at the *Evening American,* which published it a few days later.

I am sorry I did not do as well as everyone expected me to, but I tried my best. We had to run the 100 meters three times inside of one hour which, I think, tired all of us quite a bit. We had a terribly warm day for the meet, which made it hard for those who were not used to such weather.

I thought it was wonderful the way the people turned out to see us off and also thought it very wonderful of the Chicago Evening American to wish me luck through the Newark Evening News. I appreciated it very much.

I am going to train hard and I think I will be able to work up to my record time again because the time for the final was slow compared to what I have done.

I promise you I will train harder than ever to win in the Olympics because I know now what it is to have keen competition and to be beaten.

Hoping to do better and to hear from you, I am,

Sincerely,
Elizabeth Robinson

The *Evening American,* in its inimitable style, replied in kind with a full-page promotional piece in the edition of July 6, the day on which ground was broken for the Chicago Stadium, managing to pat its own back along with that of the athlete:

Congratulations, Betty, and good luck at Amsterdam!

She made it! Sixteen-year-old Betty Robinson has won a place in the sturdy band of girls who will strive to establish the athletic supremacy of their sex in America over the world's best in the Olympic Games at Amsterdam this month. . . . The Chicago Evening American feels privileged to a pardonable pride in its share in Betty's swift rise to national fame. For it was at the championship National AAU meet for girls, held here June 2 and under the sponsorship of this newspaper, that Betty set a girls' world record of 12 seconds flat. And more amazing, perhaps, is the fact that it was the first [outdoor] track meet in which Betty had ever appeared.

By then, Robinson was settled in New York, preparing to take on the world.

## CHAPTER 2

# Amelia Earhart Sailed Here

Newsreel heroes and heroines were plentiful in the 1920s. And nowhere were they better served than in New York, which employed a public servant for the purpose of welcoming VIPs to the city. His name was Grover Aloysius Whalen and so identified did he become with those he greeted and in whose honor he organized ticker-tape parades that he earned a measure of fame in his own right, gifted with the unofficial title of Mr. New York.

Attired in a top hat and sporting a luxuriant mustache, a dark-haired version of Uncle Pennybags from the Monopoly game, Whalen was at the center of the city's celebrity culture beginning with the end of the Great War and the return of General John (Black Jack) Pershing, commander of the American Expeditionary Force, in 1919. Other military heroes followed the designated path up lower Broadway, as did prominent heads of state, renowned explorers, daring aviators, and even athletes who achieved distinction overseas—notably golfer Bobby Jones (British Open champion) and Gertrude Ederle (first woman to swim the English Channel) in 1926.

The 1920s were, in the words of cultural historian Frederick Lewis Allen, "the ballyhoo years." America, he wrote, "had bread, but it wanted circuses." Whalen served as ringmaster, allowing the citizenry "an excuse to throw ticker tape and fragments of the Bronx telephone directory out the window." Other cities had their share of public celebrations, but New York, in advance of the stock market crash in October 1929, served as the "fountain-head of ballyhoo."[1]

If Betty Robinson was unfamiliar with the custom, she was enlightened as she awaited the start of her voyage to Amsterdam for the Olympics. On July 6, two days after she competed in the Olympic trials and settled in the Prince George Hotel in Manhattan for training and instructions, the chairman of the Mayor's Committee of Welcome (Whalen's official title) presented Amelia Earhart with a bouquet of American Beauty roses and led her and her two traveling companions to the open automobiles that were driven through the so-called Canyon of Heroes to city hall for the presentation of congratulatory medals.

Earhart had been little more than a passenger on the *Friendship*, a plane piloted by Wilmer Stulz and prepared by mechanic Louis Gordon, on the flight from Newfoundland to South Wales the previous month. Although her only job on the small aircraft was to the keep the log, she nevertheless had become the first of her sex to fly nonstop across the Atlantic and, in the bubbly summer of 1928, that was enough to inspire adulation in New York government circles. Surely, the symbolism of the day was not lost on the athletes awaiting their own moment as pioneers in a brave new world.

As it happened, the last order of a long eventful day for Earhart was an appearance at the Palace Theatre, where the stars of Broadway—Eva Le Gallienne, Helen Hayes, and Charles Winninger, who originated the role of Cap'n Andy in *Show Boat*, among them—staged a benefit for the American Olympic fund. Among the items auctioned in support of the team was a silk American flag that Earhart had carried on board the *Friendship*. The winning bid, by Winninger, was $650.

There was one other piece of business that linked the flier and the women who would march behind the Stars and Stripes later in the month. The ship that had borne Earhart and her colleagues home from Southampton, England, the SS *President Roosevelt*, was the same one that the American Olympic Committee had commissioned for the journey to Amsterdam the following week.

While the athletes bided their time in New York, enduring a heat wave that killed nine citizens over the course of two days, the United States Lines steamship was outfitted with a 160-yard running track of cork linoleum on the promenade deck, a boxing ring on the sun deck, gymnastics apparatus, mats for wrestling and fencing, rowing machines on C deck, and a makeshift canvas pool on the forward part of the main deck. Additionally, the six-meter yacht *Freda* and the eight-oared scull for the University of California crew were loaded aboard, as were the horses for the equestrian team.[2] The designation "American Olympic Teams" was painted in large white letters on its hull. This was America's most organized effort in the modern Olympics it had previously dominated largely on the basis of superior talent, and its disciplined approach was due largely to the presence of one man.

At 47, Douglas MacArthur was the youngest major general in the history of the U.S. Army and was on the fast track to becoming chief of staff. After earning medals and rising to the rank of brigadier general in World War I, he was appointed superintendent of the U.S. Military Academy, his alma mater. Among the major improvements he instigated during his years at West Point (from 1919 to 1922), in addition to a broader academic curriculum, was mandatory intramural competition among the corps. A baseball player in his days as a cadet, he summed up his belief in the power of athletics by writing, "Upon the fields of friendly strife are sown the seeds that, upon other fields, on other days, will bear the fruits of victory."[3] Modesty did not prevent him from ordering the words engraved above the entrance to the academy gymnasium.

Following two tours of duty in the Philippines, MacArthur was on leave of absence when William Prout, a former Olympic runner (1908), veteran AAU official, and a prominent banker in Boston who had been appointed president of the American Olympic Committee only the previous year, died suddenly in August 1927. An immediate search for a successor led directly to MacArthur, whose superior, Army Chief of Staff General Charles P. Summerall, recommended his junior officer in the expectation that "favorable publicity might accrue to the Army from MacArthur's participation."[4]

In the words of William Manchester, who wrote the definitive biography of MacArthur, "Like Charles de Gaulle and Winston Churchill, he had come to regard the late 1920s as a spiritual desert. He needed something to engage his attention and arouse his enthusiasm, and in mid-September 1927 an unexpected opportunity arrived."[5]

"I had never lost my keen interest in sports," MacArthur explained, "and attention had been attracted by the intramural system of athletic training which had been installed at West Point during my tour as superintendent. The system had been largely adopted by the leading colleges of the country."[6]

Energized by the offer, the general lent his administrative experience, his powers of persuasion, and his commanding presence to the task of fielding the best possible teams for the second Winter Olympics at St. Moritz and the ninth Summer Games in the Netherlands and raising the money to underwrite their efforts. Characteristically, he was front and center on the morning of July 11 when nearly three hundred competitors plus coaches, trainers, and administrators gathered at Pier 86 to board the *President Roosevelt*. The occasion could not have been more festive.

The *New York Times* estimated that as many as two thousand well-wishers, including a brass band from New Jersey, saluted the athletes as they climbed the gangplank and shook hands with MacArthur. "We have assembled the greatest team in our history," the general announced, adding that it was in such "superb condition for the great test [that] Americans can rest serene and assured."[7] Just before the ship pushed off at noon, escorted downriver by fireboats shooting plumes of water in the air, two American stowaways were uncovered.

"The team knew them and sympathized with them," Manchester wrote, "and MacArthur cried, 'Just the men I've been waiting for!' and dragged them aboard. Defying regulations was pure MacArthur. So was his next act, putting the stowaways to work scraping paint."[8]

Although the general insisted that the ship be run with military precision and established an early curfew for the female competitors, he had a soft spot for the junior members of the team. While four of the track and field performers were high school students—Anne Vrana and Jean Shiley, as well as Robinson, were 16 and Olive Hasenfus was 15—some of the swimmers and divers were younger still. Marion Gilman and Eleanor Holm were 14 and diver Dorothy Poynton celebrated her 13th birthday on the voyage.

The 1912 Olympics in Stockholm featured one swimming event (the 100-meter freestyle) and one diving contest (the platform dive) for women, and others were added with subsequent Games. The American Olympic Committee listed eighteen female swimmers and divers on its 1928 roster.

"I was Douglas MacArthur's favorite at the '28 Games," boasted Holm, who would win a gold medal in 1932 in Los Angeles and be thrown off the 1936 team en route to Berlin because of alleged transgressions. "I think it was because I was one of the youngest girls on the team. I have a picture of me sitting on his lap. MacArthur thought of us all as his broads—his little children—and he thought we were all great, and he admired us and had respect for us. . . . We all adored MacArthur. We didn't find him somber or anything. He loved all our silly little pranks."[9]

For the younger members of the team, the trip was educational. "The first night," recalled Shiley, a high jumper who earned a gold medal four years later in Los Angeles, "I was so naive that when I sat down to the table with all those knives, forks and spoons in front of me, I didn't know what to do with them. I learned very fast. It was very interesting."[10]

Like Shiley, Robinson didn't know any other members of the women's track and field team until they gathered in New York. She was the only Chicagoan to qualify. The Committee placed her in a cabin with Delores (Dee) Boeckmann and Catherine Maguire, ostensibly because they hailed from St. Louis and, as a result, constituted the entire Midwest contingent.

An outstanding all-around athlete, Boeckmann was 23. She made the team by finishing second in the 800 meters, which was not a popular event in the United States and was added to the trials only because it was on the Olympic schedule. Maguire, 22, was a two-time national high jump champion although she was no better than third in Newark. Both Boeckmann and Maguire had to pay their own expenses to the East Coast, not an uncommon experience at the time.

As genuinely surprised and overwhelmed as Robinson was at the prospect of an overseas expedition, she was comforted by the presence of Johnny Weissmuller. A three-time gold medalist at the Paris Games in 1924, he was among the most popular and charismatic of Olympic stars. He was also a Chicagoan. "He told my coach that he would see I was taken care of and would watch over me, like a chaperone," Robinson said.[11]

Many athletes took their cues from the strapping six-foot-three Weissmuller. They lined up to have their pictures taken alongside him as if to prove they, too, were full-fledged Olympians. He caused a stir even in entering the dining room, where he gave unspoken lessons on how to dress for dinner. And a formal dinner, with several courses, was served every night on the ship as if the athletes were paying customers on a European vacation.

Not that attendance at all meals was 100 percent. Maybelle Reichardt, a 21-year-old discus thrower from California, was among the first victims of unfamiliarity with the ocean. "I went by rail," she noted. "I was in bed the whole time; I was terribly sick. When I wasn't in bed, I was on the rail."[12] The experience left her vulnerable to teasing. "I can remember some of the girls would open the door [to the stateroom] to try to cheer me up and say, 'Don't worry, it's only three miles to shore. Straight down.' And that didn't make me feel any healthier."[13]

The youngsters, including the starry-eyed Robinson and Shiley, seemed to have the least difficulty in handling the rocking motion. The *President Roosevelt* weighed 13,869 tons and had been cruising the Atlantic, at an average speed of 18 knots, for six years. It was regarded as comfortable and included all the amenities associated with contemporary ocean liners.

"We were nine days on the water," Robinson said, "and I loved every minute of it."[14]

Unfortunately, the commercial ships of the era were not equipped with stabilizers. "When you sat in the middle of the dining room and looked from side to side, you see the ship go down and all you see is water," Shiley recalled, "then it goes up and all you see is sky. And it keeps doing that.

"The swimming team and the track team were on one level. I was worried about the horses on the ship. The equestrian team had their horses, and we had a five-day storm on the way over. Nobody was in the dining room."[15]

Amid the elaborate meals and such nightly diversions as movies, dances, bridge tournaments, Monte Carlo night, and a Masquerade Ball, there were serious attempts at exercise. Some of the athletes' efforts drew curious stares, none more so than the swimmers.

"There was no pool for the swimmers to work out in, so they erected a big, wooden square thing that they put a sack in," Robinson said. "There was water in it so that Johnny could tie himself to one side and swim away from it. It was like four feet bigger than he was. That's how the swimmers worked out. I'll never forget seeing Johnny in this square thing swimming away from one side and going nowhere."[16]

Of course, Weissmuller was not alone in his frustration. Other swimmers who shared the arrangement included Clarence (Buster) Crabbe, who would earn a bronze medal in the 1,500-meter freestyle, add a gold medal in the 400 four years later in Los Angeles, and then become the movie incarnation of Flash Gordon and Buck Rogers. Another member of the "kiddie pool" brigade was Jane Fauntz, a 17-year-old Chicagoan who, like Robinson, was sponsored by the Illinois Women's Athletic Club. Fauntz said:

> It was a wood pool and it was lined with canvas, a big canvas. And it was filled with salt water every day. We had to get in there and swim with the ocean doing its usual thing and the water slopping in and out. We had to swim

in place. We had a harness around us and on the other end of the harness was a long pole and on the other end of the pole was the swimming coach perched on the edge.

John was so big he had to swim cattycornered. So here we were in this harness and swimming and we had the clocks on us so we could tell how long we had to swim. And the coach kept hollering do this or do that or whatever. We were swimming in place and John was so big he nearly pulled [the coach] in a few times. The rest of us just swam normally in place for five minutes. We did that twice a day and that's all the training that we had on the way over.[17]

Although it was easier on the runners, they had their own prob-. lems. "The object was to do as much as you could to keep in shape by walking or jogging around the boat," said Nick Carter, who ran the 1,500 meters. "Having so many people in such a small place with all of them having the same idea in mind, it was pretty crowded. That was hard to do. Everybody was exercising, jogging, walking. It doesn't seem like there was ever a minute that there wasn't somebody running around that ship."[18]

For those who specialized in field events, the floating gymnasium was less accommodating. The shot-putters lost a few shots over the side when they rolled off the mats, and the discus and javelin throwers didn't even try. As for the pole vaulters, "there was no place they could go except overboard and we weren't about to turn around and pick up a stray pole vaulter or two," Fauntz said.[19]

Such limited opportunities combined with plentiful food offerings challenged the athletes' ability to remain in competitive condition. Some claimed to have gained as many as ten pounds during the voyage. While MacArthur relied on the various coaches to counter the best efforts of five chefs and keep the athletes in physical shape, he worked on their mental approach. He gave spirited pep talks wherever groups assembled, challenging them to represent their country with dignity and, better yet, victory.

"Altogether," one journalist wrote, "the general's approach to these Olympic Games was to treat them as a national crisis, a patriotic 'war without weapons.'"[20]

Shortly before the ship completed the nine-day journey and dropped anchor, MacArthur sent an aide to fetch Bud Houser, who had won the gold medal in both the shot put and discus at the Paris Games. At 26, Houser was one of the senior members of the team and a practicing dentist who had been called upon to fix some teeth on the voyage. Still, he was as nervous as a schoolboy at the prospect of a rebuke from the general.

When he reached MacArthur's quarters, Houser said, "Did I do something wrong, General?" But MacArthur shook his head no and, instead, offered the man a bowl of ice cream, then explained why he had summoned him to first class.

"The Olympic team does not have a captain," MacArthur told him, "but you have been chosen to carry the American flag in the parade at the opening and closing ceremonies. Johnny Weissmuller will carry the sign with the name of the country on it, and I'll be walking right behind you and Johnny."[21]

So the Americans had their marching orders from the man who would become only the fifth five-star general of the army and one of the most celebrated military leaders of the twentieth century. They received a final salute as they sailed down the great ship canal toward Amsterdam and passed the U.S. cruiser *Detroit*, which was leaving port after a courtesy call. A band played the national anthem while the warship's officers and crew stood at attention on deck until the *Roosevelt* was astern.

MacArthur could not have orchestrated a more stirring scene. Then again, such a theatrical touch may have been another instance of the general's motivational genius. His final message to his formidable but unarmed troops was simple and to the point.

"We are here to represent the greatest country on earth," he said. "We did not come here to lose gracefully. We came here to win—and to win decisively."[22]

# Soft Landing

As comforting as was the sight of land, the *terra* in the Netherlands was anything but *firma*. Track and field coaches and athletes discovered upon their arrival that the dire reports they had received the previous day when their ship stopped at Cherbourg, France, were, if anything, understated. The stadium built to house the signature events of the Olympics was unfinished and the track was under water.

General MacArthur's first reaction had been to wait and see for himself. "On the battlefield, never believe reports of disaster," he said colorfully. "Leave it to Dutch engineering genius to produce a proper field for the games."[1]

Alas, a close inspection led American officials to conclude those Dutch geniuses were in severe need of help. "Only a miracle can put the track into proper shape for the opening on July 29," declared Lawson Robertson, the men's track coach, nine days before the opening contest. "I never have heard of such a situation—Olympic teams arriving daily to find the stadium in such a hopelessly incomplete condition. It will be a tough job to break any records here."[2]

Because the stadium was erected in an area that had been marshland in a city located largely below sea level and subject to frequent precipitation, the track resembled a narrow tributary. While the sun shone brightly in the week before the Games and the Dutch continued to work on the surface, sinking piles and attempting to create a landfill eight lanes wide, it was kept off-limits to the athletes, who were dispatched toward practice fields in the vicinity.

Nor were the practice fields, located a few hundred yards from the stadium, high and dry. "The places to work out were like running in a plowed field," testified Nick Carter, a Southern Californian who was scheduled to run the 1,500 meters.[3]

In addition to being soft, the training facilities were crowded. On the Americans' first full day of preparation, the Associated Press reported, coaches had to appoint lookouts to warn the runners of an incoming discus or javelin. Shot-putters had to heave their shots across a small ditch after being cautioned they didn't have enough on hand to risk losing them in the water. Following an extensive search, team managers located an additional field, complete with grazing cows and goats, that belonged to city police and fire departments. Both requested reimbursement for any damage suffered by livestock.

Certainly, Amsterdam was a willing host for the Olympics. The Dutch had bid for the 1920 and 1924 Games before they were awarded the honor in 1928. Antwerp, Belgium, was chosen in 1920 for all it had suffered during the World War, and Paris staged the 1924 event at least in part as a tribute to Baron Pierre de Coubertin, the founder of the modern Olympics and outgoing president of the International Olympic Committee.

The Dutch were prepared to put their imprint on the Games from the outset. They made plans for an Olympic flame to burn high above the stadium for the duration of the competition. The parade of nations at the opening ceremony would begin with Greece, site of the ancient Olympic Games, and conclude with the host nation, starting a tradition that continues today. The Amsterdam Olympics would even welcome a commercial sponsor, Coca-Cola, which shipped 1,000 cases of the soft drink with the American team for sale at a stadium concession stand.

Before construction could begin on the Olympic Stadium, designed by Dutch architect Jan Wils, the area had to be raised with 750,000 cubic meters of sand. Work began on the foundation in October 1926, and the ceremonial first stone was placed by Prince Hendrik, consort of Queen Wilhelmina, in May 1927. Although the seating capacity was a modest 31,600, the structure was sufficiently large to house a football pitch rimmed by a 400-meter running track encircled by a steeply banked 500-meter cycling track. Crowds upwards of 40,000 could be accommodated with standing room admission.

But it was the running track, whose distance became the standard for international competitions thereafter, which presented the greatest challenge. Even after groundskeepers deemed it ready, athletes had their doubts.

"It was chopped up red brick dust, a very peculiar track," said Anne Vrana, a contestant in the women's 100 meters. "The footing was very, very bad because it got kind of soggy and it would kind of dig holes and you wouldn't have any backing on there."[4]

To Frank Wykoff (the teenaged sprinter who had dethroned 1920 Olympic champion Charley Paddock in the U.S. trials at Cambridge, Massachusetts) and his personal coach, it was just one more instance of poor planning. Like several other nations, including Italy and Finland, the American contingent was spending the Olympics on board the ship that delivered it to the Netherlands. An Olympic village wasn't financially feasible, and there weren't enough hotel rooms in Amsterdam to house the approximately three thousand athletes and their support staffs gathered there for the Games—let alone spectators.

"If there is anything that will ruin a track man's legs, it's running up and down stairs," suggested Norm Hayhurst, who had coached Wykoff at Glendale High School in California. "To reach the launches to go to Amsterdam the boys were forced to climb up and down four flights every time. . . . I wanted to take Frank off the boat to a hotel in Amsterdam but they wouldn't let me. Whenever I take a team away for an overnight stay believe me, I always get a hotel with an elevator. Stairs will ruin any runner's legs."[5]

The man also complained about the crowded quarters on ship, the "banquets" served every night, and the noxious smell of the stagnant water. "I think most of the Americans had 'sea legs' all the time they were there," Hayhurst complained afterward. "[The boat] was tied up in the canal. Every time we went into town, it meant a twenty minute launch ride to and from the shore through that nauseating sewage in the canal."[6]

Of course, many of the athletes not only adapted well to life on the *President Roosevelt* but some appeared to enjoy it. That group included Maybelle Reichardt, the discus thrower who was seasick for much of the voyage.

"They had American food and everything we were accustomed to," she explained. "And when we were on the ship such a long time, why, we just knew what to expect. They had made everything as comfortable as they possibly could, so we had no problems that way."[7]

As Betty Robinson herself would recall in later years, "I didn't want it to end. We all got to know each other. We became a team on that ship."[8]

On Saturday, July 28, following an early morning downpour, the entire American contingent was treated to a buffet luncheon on the hurricane deck of the ship at 11:15 A.M. Then they departed for the opening ceremony. The queen had other plans. Her Royal Highness became the first head of state to not officiate at an Olympic opening ceremony. Several theories were attributed to her absence, among them that she refused to return early from a holiday in Norway because she had not been consulted about the starting date, that she was upset that competition would be held on Sunday, even that she thought the whole affair some kind of pagan carnival.

The queen did not publicly address the issue. She simply deputized Prince Hendrik to do the honors. Wilhelmina did attend several events during the second week of the Games, and she hosted a grand dinner at the palace and distributed the gold medals on the final day of the Olympics.

As scripted by the International Olympic Committee, the prince's horse-drawn carriage arrived at the stadium and he took his place in the Royal Box at 2 P.M. The teams, which had lined up outside the entrance tunnel in alphabetical order, promptly started inside. The United States, Verenigde Staten in the Dutch language, was sixth from last. Houser recalled:

> I was watching [the other teams] march in and I noticed that most all of the flag bearers, when they passed the royal box, would dip their flags. Some even dragged them to the ground. I called General MacArthur over to see that and to ask him what I should do.
>
> He answered me by asking, "Well, Bud, how does the flag look best to you?" I told him that I liked it straight up in the air and he said, "You keep it straight up and, if you get in any trouble, I'll be right with you." So that's what I did.[9]

Olympic protocol dictated that the athlete carrying the flag dip it to a horizontal line on a level with the chest when passing the designated head of state, but the Americans had declined on several previous occasions, starting at the 1908 London Games when Edward VII opened the proceedings. Clearly, MacArthur was in agreement with the declaration that the American flag bows to no earthly king.

So Houser, marching behind standard-bearer Johnny Weissmuller and directly in front of the general, proudly held the Stars and Stripes aloft. "Johnny and I turned our eyes to the right when we walked by the prince, and General MacArthur turned eyes right and saluted, but we didn't dip the flag. . . . A lot of people over there thought we didn't have any manners, but that wasn't the point. It was just a tradition that we Americans don't dip the flag for any ruler. Well that caused quite a flap."[10]

Yet it paled in comparison to the actions of the French, who boycotted the parade altogether because they had been rebuffed in an attempt to enter the stadium the previous day in such rude fashion that a fistfight ensued between a security guard and team officials. When they returned for the opening ceremony, they said, not only was the same guard still on duty but he insisted on disparaging their nationality.

Because the stadium had been restricted while workmen rushed to apply the finishing touches, it was the first time inside for the vast majority of athletes. The overflow crowd inside—there were estimated to be another 75,000 outside unable to secure admission—was a source of amazement to Robinson and her female teammates, who were accustomed to small gatherings for their meets, and a reminder of how big the Olympics had become on the world stage.

The Dutch Royal Military Band and the Band of Royal Marines supplied the music, enhanced by 1,200 vocalists enlisted from choral groups throughout the country. The teams provided the color with their parade uniforms, ranging from the Irish in green jackets and the Swiss in crimson to the Dutch in orange. The American males were outfitted in blue blazers, white pants and straw hats while the females, 39 in an overall cast of 300, wore white from hats to shoes.

Even the homing pigeons were dressed for the occasion. Sent aloft to the sound of bugles and gunfire after speeches from representatives of the Netherlands Olympic Organizing Committee and the official opening by Prince Hendrik, they sported bands featuring the national colors of all the competing countries. While they filled the air space over the stadium, Henri Denis of the Dutch football team took the Olympic oath on behalf of all athletes. Then, as the combined choir sang "Holland's Glorie," the participants marched out while waving to friends and family in the stands.

"It was a marvelous thing to see all these countries lined up and march out on that field," Carter observed. "It was the first time I had been on the field. The first time I had been in a stadium where they had the Olympics, as a matter of fact. And to see this thing that I had been hearing about all my life. Actually being there, and a part of it, was a thrill. . . . The stands wouldn't hold any more people. It was a marvelous exhibition. It was very colorful."[11]

The good feeling among the American team carried over into the first day of competition when the United States triumphed in two of the three finals contested in track and field. John Kuck of Kansas and Herman Brix of Washington were one and two in the shot put with Kuck surpassing the world record previously held by bronze medalist Emil Herschfeld of Germany, whose country had been banned from the previous two Olympics because of its actions in the World War. Robert King of Stanford University was the other American to gain an Olympic title, in the high jump.

Although the United States didn't have a serious contender in the third championship of the day, the 10,000-meter run, it turned out to be one of the highlights of the Games. Even MacArthur thrilled at the sight of the legendary Finn, Paavo Nurmi, overtaking his countryman, Willie Ritola, in the final strides and securing his ninth, and final, gold medal in a career that spanned three Olympiads.

"It's worth crossing the ocean just to see this," declared the general, who abandoned the officials' box to a position overlooking the finish line before Nurmi crossed into history.[12]

MacArthur had several reasons to feel elated. All four U.S. entrants in the men's 100-meter dash and men's 800-meter run, as well as America's two favorites in the men's 400-meter hurdles, advanced in preliminary heats. At the end of the day, his team held an eighteen-point lead over the closest competitor, Finland, and the prospects for Monday were nothing but encouraging. The only clouds on the horizon were, well, the clouds that had settled over Amsterdam since the morning of the opening ceremony.

Monday also marked the debut of women's track and field at the Olympics with the preliminary and semifinal heats of the 100 meters. But by the time Robinson and her teammates stepped onto the cinders for the first time, the fortunes of the United States were sinking. According to the Associated Press, America "experienced one of the worst series of track and field setbacks it has ever known."[13] The fall began in the 400-meter hurdles, where British Lord David George Brownlow Cecil Burghley, who had finished third behind defending champion Morgan Taylor and Frank Cuhel in their semifinal heat on Sunday, inexplicably beat both Americans to the tape in the final. Off to a terrible start, Cuhel almost made up the five yards he lost at the outset but did manage to overcome Taylor, the world-record holder, who was well off his best form. It marked the first time the United States had lost the event in an Olympics and provided the spectators with the unlikely spectacle of an English nobleman joyously carried off the field by his commoner teammates.

Just as stunning was the experience of the United States in the 100 meters, where it had never finished worse than second. But Henry Russell and Claude Bracey were eliminated in the semifinal heats and the favored Wykoff barely survived with a third-place finish in the second race of the day. That left American fortunes up to Bob McAllister, the New Yorker known as the "Flying Cop." McAllister had won the first semifinal heat in impressive fashion and appeared capable of defending America's honor in the final.

Neither he nor the American coaches paid much attention to Percy Williams, a tall Canadian who weighed in at a frail-looking 126 pounds. Although the 20-year-old Williams had won his first two heats, he had trailed McAllister in the semifinal and did not look capable of another maximum effort two hours later. The possibility seemed particularly unlikely when the youngster from Vancouver lined up alongside the strapping, 200-pound Jack London, a native of Guyana representing Great Britain, at the start.

Wilfred Legg of South Africa broke early and was charged with a false start. Seconds later, Wykoff, his confidence shaken, did the same. When the race finally got under way, Williams immediately took command and maintained his lead throughout, holding off a late rush by London and Georg Lammers of Germany in the relatively slow time of 10.8 seconds. Wykoff struggled home fourth and McAllister, who pulled a tendon in the final 20 meters while attempting to accelerate, limped home sixth and last.

That followed a surprising result in the hammer throw where Patrick O'Callaghan, a medical doctor from County Cork, Ireland, ended an American streak of six successive Olympic victories in the field event. Expected to add three gold medals on the second day of competition, the United States gained none.

In a lead *New York Times* story, reporter Wythe Williams wrote, "'What's the matter with the American Olympic team?' was the question loudly and repeatedly asked at the close of today's stadium events, which resulted more disastrously for American athletes than ever before in the history of the Olympics."[14]

It wasn't just journalists who were mulling the question. U.S. competitors in other sports were offering opinions. "It seems as though the stadium track is not suitable for our runners," wrote Louis Nixdorff, a member of the lacrosse team who was keeping a daily journal of the trip. "It is slow and rather heavy, and the foreigners are more used to it than we are. I think one of our greatest troubles is the fact that everybody consumed so much food."[15]

Even the women, while barely making a toehold in Olympic track competition, were not spared critical judgment. According to the Associated Press, "American girls, participating in the first women's track and field event, fared little better than the men."[16]

That's because three of the four U.S. entries in the women's 100 meters (among a field of 31 representing 12 nations) failed to advance to Tuesday's final. Anne Vrana was eliminated in the first round when she finished third in a preliminary heat won by Kinue Hitomi of Japan. Mary Washburn and Elta Cartwright each qualified for the semifinals but they ran fifth and fourth, respectively, in the second round of competition. It was a particularly disappointing conclusion for Cartwright, the experienced American champion who became sick on the voyage to the continent and did not fully recover in time for her event.

Only one American, 16-year-old Betty Robinson, survived the test of stamina and nerves to reach the final. She was second behind Fanny Rosenfeld of Canada in the preliminary heat and edged Myrtle Cook, another Canadian sprinter, in the second semifinal. She alone provided a small ray of sunshine on an otherwise gloomy afternoon in the Netherlands. She alone would represent the United States in the first female track event of the modern Olympics against three Canadians and two Germans.

CHAPTER 4

# Golden Girl

Much to her own surprise, Betty Robinson slept soundly on the night before her Olympic final. She remained relaxed through what had become the daily morning downpour. She was calm throughout the ride on the water taxi and then the bus to the stadium.

Of course, she had every right to be nervous and she exercised that right the moment she arrived at the Olympic Stadium on the afternoon of Tuesday, July 31. Armed with two pairs of spikes, she took one from the changing room down to the track for a test run, only to realize she had outfitted herself with two left shoes. Her first race of the day involved a quick dash upstairs.

Consider that she was 23 days shy of her 17th birthday, was attempting to sprint 100 meters for only the eighth time in her life, and was the lone American entered in the most eagerly anticipated women's footrace in history. Robinson was flanked by three Canadians—all of them older, all of them more experienced, all of them serious contenders for the first Olympic gold medal to be awarded a woman in track—and two Germans.

She had become familiar with the Canadians during the heats on Monday, finishing a whisker behind Fanny Rosenfeld in the preliminary round and a beat ahead of Myrtle Cook in the semifinal. The two were among the foremost female athletes of the era.

A Toronto native, Cook, 26, had excelled in ice hockey, basketball, bowling, and cycling for a decade before getting the opportunity to compete in the Olympics. She had demonstrated her fitness for track by equaling Robinson's unofficial world record of 12 seconds for 100 meters at the Canadian trials in Halifax, Nova Scotia, on July 2. The 24-year-old Rosenfeld, whose family moved from Russia to Barrie, Ontario, when she was an infant, had led ice hockey, basketball, and softball teams to championships and even found time to win the Toronto Ladies Grass Court Tennis Championship while starring in track, where she temporarily shared the world record for the 100-yard dash. Ethel Smith, 21, was the Canadian champion at 200 meters in 1927.

Along with a fourth sprinter, Jane Bell, who just missed qualifying for the finals, 800-meter world-record holder Jean Thompson, and high jumper Ethel Catherwood, they constituted the country's entire female delegation. The Canadian press dubbed them "The Matchless Six," and they fully expected to dominate the competition in Amsterdam, where they were among the favorites in four of the five events.

Only in the discus did Canada lack a contender, and Poland's Halina Kanopacka took charge of that competition, which was decided shortly before the 100-meter final. Kanopacka defeated Lillian Copeland of the United States for the first Olympic gold medal awarded to a woman in track and field, with a world record throw of 129 feet, 11¾ inches. Copeland, the silver medalist, was the only other non-European to advance to the final. The other American entries, Maybelle Reichardt, Rena MacDonald, and Margaret Jenkins, were eliminated in the qualifying round.

Bolstered by her showing in the semifinal heat, Robinson was confident that she had the speed to run with the Canadians. "I knew I was going to give my opponents all that I had and if that wasn't good enough then I would have nothing to cry about," she said. "Probably I was determined to win because so many of our boys and girls had such bad luck in their events. That may have been what it was.

"In my first heat of the 100 meters, I finished second. For some reason I couldn't get away to a good start. My legs seemed tired and they wouldn't move. This feeling was gone when I won the semifinal heat and right then and there I decided I wasn't going to be nervous about anything."[1]

Well, the business with the shoes proved only that she was human. And it didn't allow her time to dwell on what could go wrong as she approached the start, which held the key to the race. It was there that lack of experience hampered her the most and where her coaches were wary of making a change that might inhibit her natural ability. As it developed, the start undid two of her seasoned rivals, Cook and Leni Schmidt, the 21-year-old German star who had won the third semifinal heat the previous day.

In its official post-Games report, the Canadian Olympic Committee identified Cook as "highly strung." Indeed, it was the oldest competitor in the race whose nerves betrayed her the most.

"The 100 meter dash for women was by far the most interesting event on the program, in as much as it provided, aside from the race itself, other scenes entirely feminine, and never before witnessed in any Olympic stadium," wrote New York Times correspondent Wythe Williams. One of those scenes was the hugging and kissing of the three Canadian finalists before they dug toeholds in their respective lanes. Wythe described a chaotic beginning to the race:

Six girls were at the starting line when the event was called. All were extremely nervous and jumpy, several breaking ahead of the gun. Myrtle Cook of Canada, the second favorite, a slight, attractive lass wearing red shorts and a white silk blouse, then made a second break. Under the Olympic rules she was disqualified.

When the starter waved her out, she seemed not to comprehend for a moment and then burst into tears. She soon had company on the sidelines when Fräulein Schmidt, a buxom German blonde, also made a second break. But instead of tears, the German girl shook her fist under the starter's nose and the spectators for the moment thought she might stage a face-scratching and hair-pulling act.

The harassed official backed away, waving the irate sprinter off the track, at the same time trying to comfort Myrtle Cook, who had sat down too near the starting line and was sobbing lustily. The starter, fearing the bad effect on the other girls, succeeded in getting the Canadian girl removed to a pile of cushions on the grass, where she remained, her head buried in her arms and her body shaking with sobs, for at least half an hour.[2]

With four runners remaining, Robinson had only to beat one to secure a medal, and the second German, Erna Steinberg, was younger and less accomplished than the American. Still, as she awaited what everyone hoped would be a fair start, Robinson was focused on only one opponent, Fanny Rosenfeld.

"It was very nerve-wracking," she said, "but I had the feeling that if I got Fanny on my right side so I knew where she was all the time, it would help. That's where I got her."[3]

Robinson was in lane five, Rosenfeld in six. Both Smith and Steinberg, the long shots, were inside them. Smith broke first but Robinson reeled her in and passed her after approximately 30 meters. When Rosenfeld moved up on the outside, the leading pair quickly drew clear of the others and staged a head-to-head duel to the wire over the final half of the race.

At 24, William Shirer was only seven years and six months older than Robinson. A Chicago native, he had sailed to Europe on a freighter after graduating from Coe College in Iowa and achieved employment as European correspondent for the *Chicago Tribune*. In ensuing decades Shirer would gain fame for his books tracing the buildup and aftermath of World War II—*Berlin Diary* and *The Rise and Fall of the Third Reich*—but on July 31, 1928, he was the lone Chicago journalist to witness Robinson's victory.

"Halfway down the lane," Shirer wrote, "she pulled up on even terms with Fanny Rosenfeld, the Canadian champion, and, going stronger with each stride, gained a foot advantage, which she held as she breasted the tape. . . . Pretty and blonde, with the air and spirits of any American high school girl, she told the correspondents of how she happened to be a sprinter."

The finish was close, close enough for a photo finish had the technology existed at the time. The Canadians thought Rosenfeld had won and they filed a protest, risking the customary charge of $5. They acknowledged that the German official, who was judging first place, had picked Robinson, but so had the French official whose assignment it was to select the second-place finisher.

Nonetheless, the decision was upheld. Robinson was credited with the time of 12.2 seconds, bettering the recognized world record of 12.4 seconds established by Gundel Wittmann of Germany in 1926, and Rosenfeld was clocked at 12.3. Smith, the other Canadian in the race, earned the bronze medal.

According to the Associated Press, Robinson's victory served as an antidote to the failure of her male track teammates. "Where the American men had been failing dismally, Miss Robinson, the only Yankee to reach the women's sprint final, ran a beautiful race to beat two Canadians and one German rival," the AP reported. "Bobbed hair flying to the breezes, the Chicago girl sped down the straightaway flashing a great closing spurt to beat the Canadian favorite, Fanny Rosenfeld, by two feet."[4]

While the margin between the runners was a matter of debate or perhaps bias, the faces of the women at the finish told a story of its own. Rosenfeld's was strained by the effort, Robinson's was wreathed in a smile of satisfaction. In the words of Knute Rockne, the celebrated Notre Dame football coach who attended the Games and wrote his observations for several American newspapers, Robinson "fairly flew down the stretch, surprising all the Americans."[5] When she hit the tape, both feet were off the ground and her arms were raised in triumph.

"I can remember breaking the tape," she recalled some six decades later, "but I wasn't sure that I'd won. It was so close. But my friends in the stands jumped over the railing and came down and put their arms around me, and then I knew I had won. Then, when they raised the flag I cried. Even today when I watch the Olympics and see the flag go up, I get so thrilled that I get the same duck bumps just thinking about it. It's something you never forget."[6]

As the flag was raised, a Dutch band played "The Star-Spangled Banner."

"I was so thrilled at having won and so pleased that I was there and all the people were singing because I had won," Robinson said. "It was a wonderful sensation. I left the field alone because all of the other girls went back up in the stands. But when I walked out of the track and over to the bus, an elderly man came up and said, 'Thank you very much for winning for America.' Even when I think of it now I get duck bumps. He was so nice. He and I were the only people around. It was thrilling. I remember often how delighted I felt when he said this."[7]

Although the *Evening American* did not have a reporter on the scene, it ran what it purported to be Robinson's "own story" the following day:

> Naturally I am pleased to be the first Olympic lady champion. It gave me a tremendous thrill when the U.S. flag went up to the peak of the flagpole and the band played "The Star-Spangled Banner." I realized it was because I had beat the other girls in the 100-meter event.
>
> I never really trained much until after the Olympic trials. I never ran a real race until five months ago. But I have had a lot of coaching since then.
>
> In the race in which a new record was made, I ran as fast as I know how and I won. Perhaps I am lucky because the Canadian runner, Miss Cook, was disqualified. I know she is good. I felt sorry for her, but I am glad I had no harder competition than I did. . . .
>
> The only thing that ruined my happiness was the fact that Helen Filkey, my friend, lost her chance to go by trip-

ping [in the Olympic trials] when she had almost a sure chance of qualifying for the final heat.

Now comes my Olympic victory and I don't know what to say except that everything so far has been beyond my fondest dreams. I feel I owe particular thanks to the Evening American for the wonderful way it has helped me along, and the IWAC, too, for the assistance they have given me.

In the same edition, the newspaper congratulated Robinson and itself. Edward J. Geiger, the sports editor, wrote:

We take off our hats to this youngster, who competed in a strange country and against tried, veteran athletes. At a time when she should have weakened and faltered, she showed a stout, fighting heart and triumphed. It requires gameness to accomplish what she did and we say she has gameness. Not only has she brought honor to Chicago by her victory, but her feat gives America the distinction of scoring the first triumph in a women's track event in the history of the Olympic Games. This is the first year in which the fair sex have been given recognition, and Elizabeth Robinson has shown the way.

The American is especially proud of Elizabeth's achievement because the Evening American was the first newspaper to recognize the worth of women's athletics and the first to give proper representation.

After the failure of so many American male runners, MacArthur was almost as thrilled as Robinson with her gold medal performance. She became a favorite of the general for the duration of the Games, accompanying him to other competitions and receptions. "He drove me all around in his car," Robinson said. "I remember it being a lot of fun."[8]

In his official report to the president, MacArthur spoke of "that sparkling combination of speed and grace by Elizabeth Robinson which might have rivaled even Artemis herself on the heights of Olympus."[9] Thus did the pride of Riverdale receive a new nickname worthy of the occasion.

## Fit for a Queen

With success comes responsibility. In addition to flowers, telegrams, and other expressions of congratulations for her sensational victory in the first Olympic footrace for women, Betty Robinson received an important assignment. She was selected to anchor the U.S. team in the 4 × 400-meter relay on the last day of track and field competition, August 5.

There was no reasonable alternative for the women's track coach, Mel Sheppard, after none of the other American women had qualified for the final of the 100 meters. Sheppard was among the early Olympic heroes, a middle-distance runner who earned three gold medals at the 1908 Games in London and added a fourth in 1912 at Stockholm. He also was the coach of the New York–based Millrose Athletic Association, which was underwritten by Wanamaker's department store and practiced on a wooden track erected on the roof of the store's garage. The U.S. team included three Millrose athletes, all sprinters.

In addition to Mary Washburn, who advanced to the semifinals in the 100, Jessie Cross and Loretta McNeil were Millrose members. They had finished fifth and seventh, respectively, in the Olympic trials but also had run with Washburn on the relay team that was second to the Northern California AC in the Newark meet. They had trained together and demonstrated the kind of chemistry Sheppard decided the United States needed against the more experienced Canadians and Germans.

His decision was a bitter blow to Elta Cartwright. She had been the unquestioned star of the Olympic trials, the first woman to gain an automatic berth on the team, and she appeared to be in the prime of her career. But illness on the voyage apparently had drained her of her characteristic energy. "I just didn't run fast enough," she lamented after her loss in the semifinal heat of the 100 meters.[1]

Anne Vrana, America's other entry in the 100, was only 16 and would have another chance, maybe two. When the U.S. team began preparations for the relay on August 1, they lined up with Washburn, a student at New York University and a hurdles specialist, in the leadoff role, followed by Cross, McNeil, and the explosive but inexperienced Robinson. While they trained for their event, the U.S. men continued to stumble on the track.

In the 200 meters, which Americans had won in five of the six previous Olympics, trials winner Charlie Borah was eliminated in the quarterfinals. The celebrated Charley Paddock, twice the runner-up in the event, faded badly in a semifinal heat. And the best that Jackson Scholz, the defending champion, could do was tie Helmut Koernig for third, a position he subsequently relinquished when he declined a runoff with the German the following day.

The surprise winner, just as he had been in the 100 meters, was the slender Percy Williams of Canada. Although he was running his eighth race in four days, Williams outkicked Walter Rangeley of Great Britain for a double last achieved in the 1912 Olympic Games.

On the same program three Americans—Stephen Anderson, John Collier, and Leighton Day—chased Sydney Atkinson of South Africa across the finish line in a hotly contested 110-meter hurdles, another perceived failure. One day later, Harri Larva, a goldsmith's engraver from Paavo Nurmi's hometown, kicked past Jules Ladoumègue of France to win the 1,500 meters for Finland. The foremost U.S. hope, Nebraska farm boy Lloyd Hahn, a fifth-place finisher in the 800 meters two days earlier whose confidence bordered on arrogance, walked off the track during his preliminary heat to derisive hoots from the crowd.

The United States continued its domination of the field events when Houser, the California dentist, repeated his 1924 triumph in the discus and Sabin Carr led a 1-2-3 sweep in the pole vault.

"But even this belated success, while it brought a modicum of comfort, could not conceal the glaring fact that the American track and field team has been a great disappointment and despite the fact that it enjoys better training and living facilities and has more coaches, trainers and managers than the team of any other nation, it will perhaps be listed as the poorest team that ever represented the United States in the Olympics," the *New York Times* reported.

"All nine events which the American officials considered that they had 'sewn up' before the games began are now past history, namely the 100- and 200-meter sprints, the 110- and 400-meter hurdles, the running broad and high jumps, the discus and hammer throws and the pole vault. Of the nine, America has won four and lost five, thus proving the managerial advance dope decidedly poor."[2]

What's more, at least one opponent was taking delight in the development. Not only had English athletes accounted for two of the five gold medals expected to go to the Yanks but representatives of the British Empire, including Canada and South Africa, had finished first in all five.

"We own to taking a little quiet satisfaction in the surprise expressed in American newspapers that the great $500,000 specially trained American team should have gone down before British athletes who went to Amsterdam in their casual way fresh from their occupations and with no scientific training," said an editorial in the *Daily News* of London. "If, after all, the moral should be that games are games, the ninth Olympic Games may have a memorable place in the history of sport."

A correspondent for the *Evening Standard* took pains to compare and contrast the menu for British athletes and the lavish meals offered their American counterparts on the *President Roosevelt,* paying special attention to the large amounts of ice cream available for dessert. "A good cargo of ice cream may perhaps act as ballast for the man whose business it is to put the shot," the report said, "but it must be a heavy burden to carry it in a sprint or a long-distance race. Are we perhaps to suppose that the Americans are drowning their sorrow of defeat in the only form of dissipation left to them?"[3]

The latter was a reference to Prohibition, an amendment to the Constitution that was enforced on the ship, at least among the athletes. The consumption of ice cream by Americans, according to the newspaper's correspondent, "seems to be a passion more devouring and fatal than that for alcoholic liquors."[4]

Adding salt to the wound was an Associated Press dispatch from London that expanded the comments in the *Evening Standard*. "The British team live at a hotel on shore in a beautiful airy place," it said. "They sit at long tables in a compartment surrounded almost entirely by glass and the biggest course of all is the green salad. I know of cases on the American team where some of the athletes have put on weight through eating too much. For instance, one [unnamed] swimmer now tips 15 pounds more than when he left New York."[5]

Criticism of U.S. results wasn't limited to outsiders. Ray Barbuti, who was scheduled to run the 400 meters, also took exception to his team's performances in the first five days of the competition. An outstanding running back at Syracuse University whose coaches had coerced him into running the quarter mile, he was not part of the track establishment and chafed at the excuses he heard from competitors as they returned to the ship. Nick Carter, the miler from California, recalled:

> Barbuti was very conscientious about his training. I never saw him with anybody. He was always training somewhere. When we'd come home from the stadium, he'd be in the ship looking out one of those portholes as we'd come up the ramp from our launch. He'd make fun of us, telling us that we'd come all this way, clear from the United States, to "poop out." . . . He'd say [we were] "a bunch of poop-outs." He'd make fun of us all the way up. He had

everybody so mad at him they could hardly look at him. But he was so big and strong nobody challenged him. Anyhow, he'd say, "I'm not going to poop out like you guys, I'm going to win."[6]

His faith in himself and his methods was not shared by other members of the American delegation even though he had won the 400 meters at the trials after world-record holder Emerson "Bud" Spencer pulled up. His event certainly wasn't among the nine American officials considered "sewn up" before the start of the Games.

"I was just a little nobody on that boat going over there," Barbuti said decades later. "They'd heard it was a fluke that I'd won the nationals. There were a lot of name people aboard who for years had been outstanding in their events, always in the papers and whatnot. All I was at Syracuse was basically a good relay runner. Nobody ever hears of a relay runner very much, except the relay runner himself. So I wasn't prominent at all, although I was probably as good if not better all around because of football."[7]

Barbuti finished second behind Canadian James Ball in his semifinal heat but that was by design. He had won two preliminary heats on the first day of competition and wanted to save himself for the final in the late afternoon of August 3. "You have to understand that there was only one more [individual running] event after the 400 meters, and that was the marathon," Barbuti noted, "and the American officials were a little concerned over what they were going to tell the American people about why this high-powered track team with all its record-holders weren't living up to expectations."[8]

They were concerned enough that Douglas MacArthur himself paid a visit to the dressing room where Barbuti was resting. "I'm lying there on the rubbing table," the runner recalled, "and he walks over to me. 'Barbuti,' he says, 'you know how important it is to us to win this race?'

"I told him, 'General, it's more important to me than it is to anybody else. I waited a long time for this.'

"He said, 'Well, you just got beat in the semifinals.'

*51*

"I said, 'Don't worry about that guy. If all I got to worry about is him, I'm home. I can take him.'"[9]

Although correct in his assessment, he didn't leave much margin for error. Off a fast pace set by the other American in the field, Herman Phillips, Barbuti impatiently began his finishing kick with 100 meters to go after being instructed to wait another 30 meters. The move caught Ball by surprise but he quickly closed to within a foot.

"I never noticed the other runners after the start," the champion told reporters afterward. "I heard them but all I kept thinking was 'run, kid, run.' I don't remember anything of the last 100 meters except a mad desire to get to that tape. It seemed a mile off when I guess I was only 50 meters from it. . . . I wanted to see the Stars and Stripes go up that middle pole so bad I felt like going out and raising it myself."[10]

Ball made the mistake of turning to see his opponent just as Barbuti lunged. For his slide across the soggy cinders, the winner suffered scrapes on his arm, leg, and side. But the doctor who attended him said they were superficial. Nevertheless, on his way back to the boat, Barbuti stopped to fill his own prescription.

"Everybody seemed to disappear when the race was over," he recalled, "and I was left to my own resources. I said, 'The hell with it.' I hired a cab and I told the driver to stop someplace where I could buy some gin. So I bought me a big crock of gin and a case of beer, and I sat in the cab and rode around and got back to the boat kind of late."[11]

Within minutes, MacArthur was in Barbuti's cabin. The runner thought his active participation in the Olympics was over. The general had other ideas. He reminded Barbuti that the preliminary heats for the 4 × 400-meter relay began the next day and he expected Barbuti to run anchor for the U.S. team. Actually, according to Barbuti, MacArthur ordered him to do so until the runner reminded the general he wasn't in the army.

MacArthur adopted a conciliatory tone and appealed to Barbuti's sense of duty. The former captain of the Syracuse football team said he'd agree if the general personally informed the runner the coaches had decided to bump from the relay that it was a command decision and not Barbuti's choice. MacArthur then summoned John Lewis and told him in Barbuti's presence.

When the American quarter milers lined up in the midst of a downpour the following afternoon, the order was George Baird, Fred Alderman, Bud Spencer, and Barbuti. Spencer ran the fastest leg on the rain-soaked track, allowing Barbuti to coast home eight yards in front of rival Jimmy Ball of Canada. Both teams advanced to the final along with the leading two finishers in each of the other heats—Germany, Sweden, Britain, and France.

Robinson and her new team also triumphed in their heat of the women's 4 × 100-meter relay, although the United States trailed Germany halfway through the race and Robinson was pushed to the finish. The American time of 49.8 seconds tied the existing world record. But the Canadians, still smarting from the results of the 100-meter race, sliced two-fifths of a second off that mark in easily outdistancing the Dutch women.

Along with the men's 4 × 100-meter team of Frank Wykoff, Jimmy Quinn, Charley Borah, and Henry Russell, they represented the United States on the final day of track and field competition, which was centered around the marathon. American Joie Ray ran well in the latter event, leading at the midway point before finishing fifth behind surprise winner Boughera El Ouafi of France, but the Yanks derived their greatest satisfaction from the relays.

While Canada did itself proud in the women's events, where the favored Ethel Catherwood won the high jump and Fanny Rosenfeld led the women's 4 × 100 team to victory in the world record time of 48.4 seconds, shattering its mark set the previous day by a full second, the United States asserted its strength on both fronts. Mildred Wiley of Taunton, Massachusetts, earned a bronze medal in the high jump, and the relay team, anchored by Robinson, also slashed a full second off its previous effort in claiming second place.

Myrtle Cook, who sat by the side of the track and sobbed after being disqualified in the 100-meter race five days earlier, was given the honor of running the final leg for Canada and nearly drifted beyond the exchange point as she impatiently waited for the baton with an eight-yard margin. To Robinson's credit, she made up half the distance by which she trailed Cook at the start of the anchor leg but the Americans had to settle for the silver medal and the time of 48.8, edging the Germans by two-tenths of a second.

"I made up some time," Robinson said, "but I couldn't catch her. The lead was too big."[12]

In the men's 4 × 100 relay, the Americans finally lived up to their potential, leading from start to finish—although anchor Russell, the intercollegiate champion from Cornell, was pressed to the finish by Helmut Koernig of Germany. The U.S. time of 41.0 equaled the world record set by the American team at the 1924 Olympics in Paris.

Even more impressive was the performance of the 4 × 400-meter team, which smashed the world mark by 1.8 seconds. The decision by MacArthur and the U.S. coaches to add Barbuti proved wise when the man pulled away from Hermann Engelhard of Germany in the stretch to win by approximately four yards.

Wythe Williams summed up the Americans' track and field performance in the August 6 edition of the *New York Times:*

> Thus the United States team managed on the last day
> of the stadium program to somewhat even up for the
> surprise drubbings received earlier in the week. The total
> results of the athletic program in both men's and women's
> divisions give the United States nine firsts, eight seconds
> and eight thirds. Finland was second with five firsts, five
> seconds and four thirds. Canada had four firsts, two
> seconds and one third. England had two firsts while the
> other representatives of the British Empire, namely Ireland
> and South Africa, had one each. Poland also had one first,
> likewise Germany, both of which were for women's events.
>
> Germany before the games was considered the strongest
> team next to the United States. On the complete showing
> it is seen, by counting in the one women's event won by

the United States, that General MacArthur was correct in his advance calculations as to the number of times the Stars and Stripes would be hoisted on the center mast.

Another week remained in the competition. While Robinson toured Amsterdam's museums, canals, and flower markets, American athletes would triumph in many disciplines. Johnny Weissmuller would burnish his image as one of the most celebrated athletes on earth with two more gold medals in swimming. Pint-sized Ulise (Pete) Desjardins, a student at Stanford, would become the first male diver in Olympic history to win both the springboard and platform events. And the United States outscored all other countries by a comfortable margin, accounting for 22 gold medals and 17 Olympic records in 109 events.

Those gold medals were personally awarded by the queen at the closing ceremony on August 12. Her husband, the prince, presented the silver medals, and Count Henri Baillet-Latour, the president of the IOC, dispensed the bronze medals from the royal box at the stadium.

"Nothing has been more characteristic of the genius of the American people than is their genius for athletics," MacArthur wrote in his official report prepared on the voyage back home. "Nothing is more synonymous of our national success than is our national success in athletics. If I were required to indicate today that element of American life which is most characteristic of our nationality, my finger would unerringly point to our athletic escutcheon."[13]

The general was particularly complimentary of two athletes, the only two to win individual events in track, the historic heart of Olympic Games dating back to the ancient Greeks. While he listed all the gold medal winners in his report to President Calvin Coolidge, he singled out the teenaged girl from Illinois and the tough middle-distance runner from Syracuse for lavish praise. So did MacArthur, inadvertently or otherwise, appoint an unlikely king for the U.S. team to pair with its radiant homecoming queen, Betty Robinson.

# CHAPTER 6

## New York

For her first athletic endeavor on American soil as the world's fastest female runner, Betty Robinson raced down the gangplank onto Pier 84 and leaped into the waiting arms of her father, Harry, then whirled to embrace her mother, Elizabeth. Exactly forty-two days after sailing to Europe, the neophyte sprinter returned with an Olympic gold medal and weeks of pent-up emotion.

"When they parted," noted the *Chicago Tribune* reporter on the scene, "tears were rolling down Elizabeth's cheeks and when somebody of course asked what she was crying about, she said, 'I don't know. I'm just so happy.'"

For the record, the reporter was Westbrook Pegler, the newspaper's national correspondent and a future columnist of some note.

Although rain did alter the schedule for welcoming the U.S. Olympic team back from Amsterdam—starting with Grover Whalen's selection of a fedora in place of his formal top hat—it didn't dampen Robinson's joy at being reunited with her parents. They had caught their first glimpse of her from the water. Relatives and close friends of team members had been invited to board the mayor's boat, *Macom,* and the tug *Manhattan* at the Battery early in the morning and accompany the SS *President Roosevelt* through the New York harbor to its berth.

There was a band on each of the smaller vessels, and they greeted the Olympians with "The Star-Spangled Banner" and "Home, Sweet Home." Roars arose from the *Roosevelt,* where the athletes were standing on deck in their dress uniforms, as the ship passed the Statue of Liberty. Other ships sounded sirens and whistles, and fireboats sprayed geysers of water into the air. Hundreds watched the *Roosevelt* tie up at the pier, their numbers suddenly reinforced by passengers from the *Macom* and the *Manhattan.*

In counterpoint to Robinson's teary dissolve, Ray Barbuti disembarked with the inner fire that stoked his surprise victory in the 400 meters. Still smarting from the excuses and complaints of failing teammates, he told reporters, "Of course, there was squawking. Nobody likes to lose, and when we lost races, we naturally squawked. Don't ever let anybody tell you that the color of a man's jersey or his flag makes any difference in his sportsmanship. Winners are the only ones who never squawk."[1]

Barbuti was equally outspoken about the charges that U.S. athletes were overfed and undertrained, as symbolized by the ice cream diaries.

"What about the ice cream?" he said unapologetically. "Of course, we ate ice cream. The coaches couldn't be around snooping like a bunch of boarding house landladies to see how much each man ate. What difference does an extra plate of ice cream make on a hard-bellied six-foot swimmer? Europeans drink wine. We eat ice cream."[2]

The original plan was for the Olympians, once they had cleared customs, to board the *Macom* and *Manhattan* and sail down to the Battery for the start of a parade to city hall. The inclement weather changed all that. Instead of Mayor James J. Walker awaiting the athletes in his office, he was driven to the pier, leaving behind a crowd of some 1,500 and a delegation of 50 police officers at City Hall Park.

At the approach of the dapper mayor, whose friendship with celebrities and familiarity with the city's nightlife had earned him the nickname "Beau James," the fire department band struck up "The Sidewalks of New York," and Whalen introduced His Honor. "We have welcomed many distinguished visitors," Walker said, "but on no previous occasion have I felt the genuine pleasure of welcoming on behalf of the people of New York the best we have in all our land.

"Your victory is enhanced by the accomplishments of the girls, which shows pretty well what a well-balanced nation America is. May you always be an inspiration to those of us who stay at home. You went over to do your job and you did it well. American perseverance coupled with American enthusiasm has again won the admiration of the world."[3]

The mayor then presented medals bearing the seal of New York to members of the team, calling them individually to a makeshift platform. Two of the loudest ovations were for Robinson and Barbuti, the only individual winners in track. Following the ceremony, Walker autographed the wooden shoes Robinson had purchased as souvenirs in Holland and had signed by her teammates.

The next order of business was an official welcome-home luncheon at the Hotel McAlpin on Herald Square, after which the secretary of the American Olympic Committee, Joseph Reilly, declared the team officially disbanded. In between, photographers for New York's many newspapers and wire services commanded publicity shots from the athletes, among them a pose of Robinson being lifted into the air by Matt McGrath, the New York cop whose Olympic shot put record set in the 1912 Games of Stockholm had yet to be equaled.

Although Douglas MacArthur did not attend the luncheon, following orders to report immediately to Washington, he did make public his official report to President Calvin Coolidge. Written in what popular journalist Bob Considine identified as "purple ink," it began:

Dear Mr. President:

Article X of the Constitution and Bylaws of the American Olympic Association directs the submission of a report by the American Olympic Committee on the Olympic Games. In undertaking this difficult task, I recall the passage in Plutarch wherein Thermistocles, being asked whether he would rather be Achilles or Homer, replied: 'Which would you rather be, a conqueror in the Olympic Games or the crier who proclaims who are conquerors?' And indeed to portray adequately the vividness and brilliance of that great spectacle would be worthy even of the pen of Homer himself.

No words of mine can even remotely betray such great moments as the resistless onrush of that matchless California eight as it swirled and crashed down the placid waters of the Sloten; that indomitable will for victory which marked the deathless rush of Barbuti; that sparkling combination of speed and grace by Elizabeth Robinson which might have rivaled even Artemis herself on the heights of Olympus. I can but record the bare, blunt facts, trusting that imagination will supply the magic touch to that which can never be forgotten by those who were actually present.[4]

While the athletes were traveling to New York from the east, Jimmy Corcoran was arriving from the west. The irrepressible reporter from the *Chicago Evening American* had spent the better part of the summer on the political beat, covering the presidential conventions in Kansas City (Republicans) and Houston (Democrats) that nominated Herbert Hoover and Al Smith, respectively. But now that Robinson was back in the country, Corcoran picked up the thread of the story that was so dear to his editors and readers.

Ironically, just a week before the ship came in and Corcoran came to meet it, *The Front Page* opened at the Times Square Theatre. Written by Ben Hecht and Charles MacArthur, two former Chicago newspapermen, it was a satire on the popular press based at least in part on a case involving the *Evening American*. The production was a smash hit.

If her parents were of a mind to celebrate at a Broadway show that night, Betty Robinson was in no condition to join them.

The return trip was joyous, with the training limited to the occasional jog around deck and the curfew relaxed. MacArthur set the tone by presenting each of the female pioneers with a gold charm in the shape of a globe and words of praise.

All Betty wanted was an early dinner and a comfortable bed. That left Corcoran to engage her father in conversation.

At 55, Harry Robinson was a pillar of his community. He was the longtime superintendent of the Globe Rendering Company, a director of Riverdale's first bank, and treasurer of the local Masons' lodge. Born in Carrowdore, a small village in County Down, Northern Ireland, the stocky Robinson confessed he was a superior athlete while growing up in St. Paul, Minnesota.

"I liked track in my day," he told Corcoran, "and could step with the best around our country. We haven't any boys in our family and, of course, I despaired of ever having a chance to cheer any of the youngsters in my family on the athletic field. There are three girls. Babe is the youngest.

"I never looked to one of my daughters to fulfill my desire, but here the baby of the family has done it. Just write it down that I am the happiest man in the United States."[5]

Upon awakening in her hotel room the next morning, the daughter of the happiest man in America received another distinction, one that was not commemorated with a medal. She was 17 years old.

Alas, rain fell on Babe Robinson's birthday, canceling a planned trip to Yankee Stadium to meet New York's Babe, George Herman Ruth. After some sightseeing with her parents, she attended a private dinner during which Harry Robinson informed her that her present, a combination birthday-Olympic gift, was waiting in Chicago. It was equipped with four tires and a steering wheel.

When the weather cleared the next day, Betty and her parents made the trip to the Bronx. The Yankees were scheduled to play a doubleheader versus the St. Louis Browns, and Ruth, the great slugger who had established a major-league mark of sixty home runs in 1927, was in a slump. After setting a record pace through the first four months of the season—he hit his forty-second homer on August 1—Ruth appeared virtually powerless in the following three weeks. So when a meeting was arranged between the two Babes in the Yankees' dugout, Ruth was almost contrite.

"Miss Robinson, I'm more than happy to meet you," Ruth said as reported by Corcoran, whose duties included the coverage of major-league baseball. "I've been reading about what you did for the U.S. in the Olympic Games and I want you to know this is a real pleasure."

Blushing slightly, Robinson returned the compliment. "I'm happy to know you, too, Mr. Ruth," she said. "My dad has seen you hit a lot of home runs but he would never take me to the games."

Alluding to his recent problem hitting home runs, Ruth then asked Robinson for help. "Will you teach me to run sometime?" he said.

"Sure," she replied. "But l thought you always hit home runs and never had to run."

"Seems I've been running all the time the last few days," Ruth said with a smile.[6]

He then provided a demonstration of his woes, collecting three hits in the two games, both losses, but failing to reach the fences, while she and her parents observed from box seats alongside the Yankees' dugout. Although it was speculated that Ruth said he would hit a home run for Robinson, no such conversation was reported. Such promises were frequently attached to Ruth's name whenever he encountered a celebrity or a sick child.

Ruth did hit a home run the following day against the Detroit Tigers but finished with only six for the month of August. He hit another eight in September as the Yankees held off the Philadelphia Athletics to win their third consecutive American League pennant en route to a sweep of the St. Louis Cardinals in the World Series.

The Robinsons enjoyed one more full day in New York before boarding the Broadway Limited, the Pennsylvania Railroad's signature train, on its overnight journey to Chicago.

## CHAPTER 7

---

# Parade Rest

On July 19, 1928, while the ship carrying the U.S. Olympic team was approaching the coast of Holland, Amelia Earhart and her two travel companions arrived at Union Station. As if to prove that ballyhoo was not limited to New York, Chicago had issued its own civic invitation to the first woman who flew nonstop across the Atlantic Ocean. Its rationale was that the aviatrix had graduated from Hyde Park High School in 1916 after spending her senior year at the institution located near the University of Chicago.

The reception accorded Earhart, a Kansas native who was living in Boston at the time of her historic flight, was extravagant, starting with the massive crowd that met her train and the ticker-tape parade to city hall. If nothing else, it served as a challenging dress rehearsal for the return of Betty Robinson five weeks later. With more authentic connections to the Chicago community, the Olympic champion was greeted, according to the *Chicago Tribune,* as the "conquering heroine."[1]

From the moment she stepped off a special car attached to the Broadway Limited on the morning of August 27, Robinson was engulfed by friends who knew her before the Olympics and supporters who wanted to show their appreciation for her performance in Amsterdam. In the din created by several brass bands at the station, eight teammates from the Illinois Women's Athletic Club surged forward for hugs and kisses, and Jane Wiedemann and Beatrice Sachs, classmates from Thornton Township High School, presented Robinson with a huge basket of flowers. Officials from Chicago, Riverdale, and Harvey conveyed their congratulations to the youngster decked out in her official, and by now obligatory, white Olympic dress uniform.

Flanked by her parents, Robinson tried to speak, but her attempts were invariably cut short by gasps for air and tears of joy.

"I can't say anything," she said between breathless shout-outs to faces in the crowd she recognized. "I'm so happy I can't talk. Besides, I can't seem to keep from crying."[2]

Once clear of the station, she was escorted into a waiting convertible and helped onto a perch behind the back seat. Sitting "just like 'Lindy,'"[3] according to a front-page newspaper caption, she waved at crowds lining both sides of the street as she was led through the Loop to city hall, where Mrs. William Hale Thompson, the mayor's wife, and Chicago city attorney William Saltiel officially welcomed her home. When those speeches concluded, a representative from the city of Harvey presented Robinson with a diamond-studded wristwatch.

From city hall, she was ushered back into the automobile and driven through more waiting admirers to State Street, then north toward the club where she trained for her great adventure. Following a luncheon at the IWAC, Robinson was presented with a lifetime membership and jeweled club pin by Mrs. Bessie Bragg Pierson, the club president, while her teammates fastened a slender gold chain holding a tiny gold track shoe around her neck.

"Oh, it's wonderful," she said at a reception at the edge of the seventeenth-floor pool. "It's just wonderful but I'm really much more nervous today coming home than I was on the day of the race. Ever since I got to New York I've been shaky about it—and just crazy to get here."[4]

Nor did she come empty-handed. "She brought all of her teammates a little hand-painted handkerchief as a souvenir," noted hurdler Evelyne Hall. "She was a delightful girl."[5]

Within minutes, the reception committee steered Robinson back into the car for a ride to the Edgewater Beach Club near Lake Shore Drive. There she received a silver tea set. "After that," according to the *Tribune*, "she was free to discard the little white felt hat, the white coat with the red, white and blue shield over her heart, the straight white dress and the white hose and slipper that constituted her uniform and to take a refreshing dip in the tank."[6]

Within the hour, she had to put that uniform back on for the last of the day's scheduled activities, a dinner given by the Central AAU at the Sherman Hotel, where Olympic track team manager Fred Steers proclaimed that Robinson would have shaved a fifth or even two-fifths of a second off the world record if the track in Amsterdam hadn't been so slow. After a full round of speeches and the presentation of a gold bracelet in honor of the occasion, the champion arose and said one final time, "I'm certainly very happy and thank you all."[7]

With that, Robinson was bundled into a car and driven to her Riverdale home for a long overdue rest. First, of course, she stopped to admire the snazzy roadster parked in front of the garage behind the house.

Cars would be the center of attention the next day, her first full day in the industrial suburb where she was born and raised. In the four weeks since Robinson's victory in the 100 meters, officials of Riverdale, adjacent Dolton, and surrounding communities had hatched a plan for a parade that wound throughout the area, culminating with a celebration at Riverdale Park. Since the park—located a few blocks from Robinson's house—lacked a central meeting area, a wooden gazebo was erected. The program included three bands, fireworks before and after the speeches, and a street dance for those who couldn't make it inside.

"And what a greeting, my friends," observed Jimmy Corcoran in the *Evening American*, following the story he stumbled upon at the start of June in Soldier Field all the way to its glorious conclusion on the evening of August 28, in his conversational style.

It was the night of nights for Riverdale and the entire Calumet District. It was their homecoming of the leading lady from the Illinois Women's Athletic Club. . . . Not long before Betty was due in town from Chicago for the great testimonial parade, Riverdale and Dolton were bubbling with excitement. Everyone had hurried home from work to drape the family chariot.

Dinners were hurried through so that every member of the household could roar a "hello" to Betty when she arrived. Porches were draped with red, white and blue streamers. Lanterns were hung from end to end.

Over near the Lincoln School in Dolton, which is only a hop and step from Riverdale, the boys and girls, with their necks washed clean, toddled up and down waiting for the big moment. The "grown folks" were parked along the curbs. Up the street fifteen motorcycle policemen, with their mounts snorting, waited. And then Betty arrived.

Red lights. Giant bombs. Whoops and whoopee. The Calumet had never seen anything like it before. The parade got under way at 7:20. It twined through Riverdale, Ivanhoe, West Pullman, Roseland, Kensington and back again to Riverdale. At every crossroad and every important cross section in the towns, there were cheers for Betty.

She sat high up in an open touring car. She was garbed in white, with the Olympic shield beaming on the heart side of her jacket.

In the line were 1,200 motor cars. Where did they come from? Ask Bill Reich. He was the master of ceremonies. Along the line at intervals of a block, red fire burned. A returning Lindbergh couldn't have had a more sincere or more colorful demonstration.

It was estimated that close to 20,000 gave Betty a wave as she passed along the thirteen-mile circuit. The lineup of autos was so drawn out that the head of the parade met the tail end before the latter had left Riverdale. Figure that out.

And then they had her back in the public park of her hometown. Of course the band played the national anthem while the crowd stood. Mothers raised their youngsters so they could see Uncle Sam's favorite daughter. The old heads opined as how "it was the god darndest thing I've ever seen in my day."

Of the several speakers in the park it was Edward J. Tobin, commissioner of Cook County schools, who got the greatest response when he called Robinson the Joan of Arc of Cook County. Reich, the city attorney and a family friend, had the honor of presenting her with a gift from her neighbors. In the words of Corcoran, "Her admirers in Riverdale, Dolton and Roseland grouped their little contributions and presented her with a diamond ring that was as big as a wee grape. It sparkled like Betty's eyes. Girls, it was some rock."

For the seventh or eighth time in her extended homecoming, Robinson was overwhelmed. "I appreciate all this from the bottom of my heart," she said, "and I'll never forget it."[8]

At one stage, the motorcade had passed in front of Robinson's home on East 138th Street and, when the ceremonies were over, the color guard of the local American Legion escorted the teenager they proclaimed as the "Princess of Sprint" back to the house where family and close friends awaited her.

There was an interesting postscript to the event the following morning as witnessed by Thomas Kinney, whose Boy Scout troop was assigned to help park the cars on the town baseball and football fields following the motorcade.

"The day after the program," he recalled, "Betty was driving a fancy roadster car and she made it her business to drive around town and wave to and stop to greet neighbors or friends who did not live on the parade route."[9]

Thus Robinson reached out and touched about everyone in the

village who wanted to reach out and touch her. She had one final duty to perform, an invitation to a Kiwanis club luncheon which she had accepted before her trip to the Olympics and had promised to fulfill win, lose, or tie. Accompanied by her parents and Reich, Robinson was escorted to the chamber of commerce headquarters in Harvey, where, despite the fact there had been no announcement of her appearance, she was greeted by an enthusiastic crowd.

Among the speakers was Charles Price, the teacher who "discovered" Betty Robinson running for the commuter train, and her father, who expressed his appreciation for what was being done for his "little girl." Blushing slightly, Betty Robinson then thanked everyone in attendance, particularly Mr. Price. After each of the guests offered his or her congratulations, the champion finally was free of her obligations.

The next stop was Stone Lake, Indiana, and a few days of peace and quiet at the campground where the Robinsons' extended family gathered every summer. Time to gear up for the next major test in her life, senior year at Thornton Township High School.

# Sexual Politics

With four world records in five events, with gold medals distributed among four nations, the perception—at least in the United States—was that female track and field athletes had earned themselves a permanent place in the Olympic Games.

Members of the International Olympic Committee had a different reaction. The "experiment," as they viewed it, was not a success, not with all the criticism levied after the 800-meter test. The longest race in the women's program became a flash point for opponents of female participation and threatened to sabotage the movement.

While none of the participants suffered aftereffects, the same could not be said for the event. It was another 32 years before the Olympics would allow women to run so far again, and harrowing reports of the race almost forced female athletes out of the arena altogether.

"The administrators, members of the IOC and the media apparently had decided that women were too frail to compete in a race as long as 800 meters," charged Anita DeFrantz, a 1976 Olympic rowing medalist and the first woman to serve as a vice president of the IOC's executive board. "As a result, the reports from the 1928 Games not only distorted the results of that race but in some cases completely fabricated facts to support their viewpoint."[1]

The facts were that nine women started the race, nine finished, and the winner, Lina Radke of Germany, established a world record that lasted for 16 years. But the emphasis in the media coverage was on the condition of the competitors at the finish. Even Wythe Williams of the *New York Times,* who limited his observation to a single paragraph at the end of his Olympic track story, chose to editorialize.

"The final of the women's 800-meter run," he wrote, "plainly demonstrated that even this distance makes too great a call on feminine strength. At the finish six of the nine runners were completely exhausted and fell headlong on the ground. Several had to be carried off the track. The little American girl, Miss Florence MacDonald, who made a gallant try but was outclassed, was in a half faint for several minutes, while even the sturdy Miss Hitomi of Japan, who finished second, needed attention before she was able to leave the field."[2]

Among the less restrained media organizations was the *Daily Mail* (London) which, despite the absence of any Brit from the field, chose headlines that screamed: "Women Athletes Collapse," "Fierce Strain of Olympic Race," and "Sobbing Girls."

Meanwhile, the *Times* (London) questioned the danger posed by such a strenuous race: "The half dozen prostrate and obviously distressed forms lying in the grass at the side of the track after the race may not warrant a complete condemnation of the girl athletic championships, but it certainly suggests unpleasant possibilities."[3]

Even Knute Rockne, the esteemed football coach at Notre Dame, piled on in his report for a U.S. news service.

> The half mile race for women was a terrible event. Five
> of the six girls to finish collapsed. Miss MacDonald, the
> American girl, pluckily stayed in to get sixth. It was not
> a very edifying spectacle to see a group of fine girls run
> themselves into a state of exhaustion. The event was put
> in at the insistence of the Europeans. The English trainer
> refused to allow his girls to run. The American should
> have done likewise.

If running the half mile for women is an athletic event,
they ought to include a six-day dance contest between
couples. One is as ridiculous as the other.[4]

But the report that received the most traction was one by John
R. Tunis, a Harvard man whose time as a sports writer would lead
to a renowned and lucrative career as an author of sports novels for
adolescents.

"Obviously at the present time one cannot dogmatize upon the
physical ability of women to stand the strain and stress of athletic
competition; but one can say conservatively that in competitive
sport women are far more in need of medical supervision than men,"
Tunis wrote in the aftermath of the race. "Those who doubt this
statement should have stood beside me during the eight-hundred
meter run in the Olympic Games at Amsterdam. . . . Below us on the
cinder path were eleven wretched women, five of whom dropped
out before the finish, while five collapsed after reaching the tape. I
was informed that the remaining starter collapsed in the dressing
room shortly afterward."[5]

Forget for a moment that men had traditionally been praised for
such dogged efforts in pursuit of victory and that the 800 meters is
among the most demanding in track. But Tunis managed to over-
state the numbers at the start, let alone those who fell to the track. To
Harold Abrahams, the 100-meter champion in 1924 at Paris and a
member of the official British delegation in Amsterdam, newspaper
accounts of the women's race were "sensational and grossly exaggerated." Yes, some of the participants lay down in the infield after the
race, as much in disappointment as in fatigue, he theorized, but that
was nothing less than he experienced at men's meets.[6]

"I understand that they felt that this was too long a race and that
some athletes were collapsing," recalled Anne Vrana, the American
sprinter who attended the race. "Well, they were tired. They had
run 800 meters and it was a long distance and, of course, they were
winded. But they certainly weren't collapsing all over the track the
way they described it. I was there and I saw it. They needed some

rest but they certainly weren't in terrible shape. . . . It's a shame that this legend was allowed to grow the way it was. I was there and they were winded. I'll guarantee you that, but I have seen men that were winded at the end of the 220 just as badly."[7]

One of the men standing at the finish line, Dr. Fr. M. Messerli, a physician as well as the founder and general secretary of the Swiss Olympic Committee, thought that the fuss was absurd. "One amusing little incident occurred at the Finals of the 800m flat, when reaching the winning post, two Canadians and one Japanese competitor collapsed on the lawn, the public and the journalists believed them to be in a state of exhaustion," Messerli wrote in 1952. "I was judging this particular event and on the spot at the time, I can therefore certify that there was nothing wrong with them, they burst into tears thus betraying their disappointment at having lost the race, a very feminine trait!"[8]

Consider that in a post-Olympic meet at Berlin two weeks later, Hitomi was fresh enough to win the 800 meters. The runner-up was Elfriede Wever, the German girl who was last in the Amsterdam race. In his report many years later, Messerli also noted that "we were very much interested to hear that Madame Radke, winner of the 800m, was actually married and the mother of a child."

Luke McKernan, a British film historian who studied the full-length documentary of the Amsterdam Olympics and wrote an academic paper on the contents, was amazed at what he didn't find.

"Viewed now," he wrote in 2011, "it is hard to imagine how what looks to our eyes a well-fought, routine race could have occasioned such shock and led to such a dramatic decision (just one runner collapses at the end of the race). Film can elevate, but equally its matter-of-factness can bring things down to commonplace reality—but the alarm was caused more by the reported nature of the incident than by anyone examining the documentary record that the film provided."[9]

In other words, the race was viewed through a male prism that altered, even blinded, some observers from the reality of the moment.

"It was luridly falsified versions, not the reality of what happened at the finish line in 1928, that enabled the IOC to keep the women's 800m off the program until 1960," observed Roger Robinson in the May 2012 issue of *Running Times* magazine.

The controversy was such it drove a wedge even among female athletes, forcing them to take sides. Among those who erred on the side of caution was Betty Robinson, whose four months of training as a sprinter left her ill equipped to debate the issue. Yet, upon returning to the United States, she was pressed for an opinion. In a statement she later regretted, Robinson said:

> I believe that the 220-yard dash is long enough for any girl to run. Any distance beyond that taxes the strength of a girl, even though some of them might be built "like an ox," as they sometimes say.
>
> Some of the scenes at the finish of various 800-meter races recently have been actually distressing. Imagine girls falling down before they hit the finish line or collapsing when the race is over! The laws of nature never provided a girl with the physical equipment to withstand the grueling pace of such a grind.
>
> Short distance events in girls' meets are splendid. They are not harmful. A girl can run the 50-yard dash and show no ill effect. She can do the 100 and not suffer. Nor is the 220-yard dash too much. After that, however, track authorities should draw the line. I do not profess to be an expert on heart and nerve reaction to the longer distances, but common sense will tell you that they must be quite severe.[10]

Although this was in direct contrast to the tests done by Dr. Stewart in the United States and other physicians in Europe, such "common sense" was widely accepted. The IAAF had the testimony of Dr. Messerli, who served on a commission charged with studying the question of women's participation, but many members of the IOC, particularly its president, were not open to reason.

When the IOC staged its annual meeting in 1929, it voted to remove women's track and field from the next Olympics. Remarkably, it was delegates from Canada, the country that enjoyed the most success at Amsterdam with two gold, one silver, and one bronze medal, who led the motion to drop the sport.

Fortunately for all involved, the IOC left the conduct of the individual sports to the various international federations. And the IAAF was not about to jettison the women whom it had plans to control and market for its own purposes. Gustavus T. Kirby, the president of the Amateur Athletic Union and an American representative to the IAAF, convinced the international body to threaten the withdrawal of all men's track and field athletes from the Olympics if the IOC didn't reverse its decision to ban women at its congress in Berlin in May 1930.

It was of no small importance to Kirby and his organization that the 1932 Olympics were scheduled for Los Angeles.

"In 1932 the Olympic Games will be held in Los Angeles and already the AAU is canvassing the high schools of the country for material," said Helen Smith, the director of physical education for women at the University of Cincinnati and an opponent of female participation in the Olympics. "They are not interested in seeing that every girl has a chance to take part in the Olympic Games, but they will take one or two 'star' performers, train them intensively, and boost them and America to their best ability."[11]

Smith and many of her colleagues feared that the commercialism which had overtaken men's sports in the United States would do the same for women. "The colleges and universities have succeeded in conducting a sane and wholesome program of athletics for girls," she wrote in an article, "The Evils of Sports for Women," in the January 1931 *Journal of Health and Physical Education*. "But it is the great mass of American girls who are in industry who are more likely to be injured if the present trend in men's athletics continues to seep into women's athletics."

While awaiting the decision of the IOC to the IAAF threat in May 1930, she wrote, "That such drastic measures probably will not be necessary, however, was indicated by Murray Hulbert, former president of the Amateur Athletic Union of the United States, who joined Kirby in leading the fight. Hulbert pointed out to the Associated Press that the Olympic Games in this case are to be held in the United States, which is strongly in favor of allowing the girls to compete at Los Angeles in 1932."

It was at that point, almost two full years after the 800 meters in Amsterdam, that Smith repeated the quote credited to John R. Tunis.

"And yet," she noted, "the American delegates insist on the retention of these unwholesome activities. The women of America do not want these events, and by women I mean those trained educators who have had experience in athletic coaching and training. Who then is promoting these events? A small group of men who are again interested in promotion and commercialization, and not in a sane, wholesome program for all girls and women."[12]

When the full Olympic congress assembled in Berlin, the IOC backed down. Although Baillet-Latour attempted to use the 800-meter controversy to suggest that women be allowed to compete only in "aesthetic events," which he identified as swimming, tennis, skating, and gymnastics, the committee voted by an overwhelming majority to restore women's track and field to the Games.

"Anyone who observed the exhibition put on by girl athletes in connection with the Olympic Congress in Berlin," noted Avery Brundage, Douglas MacArthur's successor as president of the American Olympic Committee, "would be a strong advocate for sports of all kinds for girls under proper supervision."[13]

Yet, as a result of the negative publicity generated by the 800, that race was removed from the Olympic program. In its place, the IAAF substituted the 100-meter hurdles. It also added the javelin for a total of six events in Los Angeles, well below the 10 events sought by the women's federation.

In fact, the Olympics failed to stage any event for women beyond 100 meters until after World War II, when a 200-meter race was added in 1948 at London. Officials didn't dare restore the 800 to the women's program until 1960 in Rome. Not that the world had forgotten what happened, or at least what many thought had happened, thirty-two years earlier in the inaugural event.

"When this race was tried at Amsterdam in 1928," decorated sports columnist Arthur Daley wrote in uncharacteristically facetious fashion, "the gals dropped in swooning heaps as if riddled by machine-gun fire. This year the event was restored. Why?"[14]

# CHAPTER 9

# Senior Moment

None of her classmates had to ask Betty Robinson what she did during her summer vacation. Those who weren't aware of her athletic emergence in the late spring certainly learned about her efforts during the long break. What with all the newspaper coverage, the welcoming parades, and word of mouth, she returned for her senior year at Thornton as the most famous student in school history.

As if to underline her importance, the *Evening American* sent a photographer to capture a typical school day for Robinson, starting with breakfast in her kitchen, moving on to a staged encounter with her "chums," and concluding with a reading assignment at her desk. In truth, there was nothing typical about any of her days at Thornton, so involved was she in extracurricular activities in addition to her recent training requirements.

Consider that in the second full week of classes, Robinson was elected president of the Girls' Club, which, among other duties, was charged with the task of mentoring freshmen. This was in addition to her role as class secretary, the only female among senior class officers, for which she was chosen the previous spring. Not only did she sing in the Girls' Glee Club but she served as its librarian. And, of course, she continued to act, taking a leading part in the Boys' and Girls' Club play *Bab,* which had starred Helen Hayes in its Broadway premiere eight years earlier, and the senior play, *It Pays to Advertise,* a screwball comedy set in 1914.

That might have been enough to exhaust any of her peers, especially one carrying an A average, but Robinson had the extra burden of practicing with the Illinois Women's Athletic Club. While the school did not sponsor a girls' track team on which to compete, people in the area still wanted to see her run at and for Thornton. So Charles Price, the man who discovered her and first nurtured her talent, and athletic director Joseph Stephens concocted a plan to please everyone.

At halftime of Thornton's first football game of the season, against Morgan Park, they staged an exhibition in which Robinson attempted to break the world record for the 100-yard dash on a track cleared alongside the gridiron. Although the distance wasn't recognized internationally, Robinson and Helen Filkey, her club mate, jointly held the accepted mark of 11.4 seconds. Running on her own, against the clock, Betty again was timed in 11.4. Then, after resting a few minutes, she ran 80 meters in 10.2, comparatively faster than her previous effort.

This occurred on the afternoon of September 29, a beautiful autumn day, after Robinson was tended a testimonial luncheon by the Thornton athletic association. Of note to all was the size of the crowd, announced as 2,300, significantly larger than any traditionally drawn to the institution's football games. According to the *Thorntonite,* the school yearbook, "A greater part of the crowd was present to see Babe Robinson run in between the halves."

And to think school officials almost blocked her participation the previous spring. "My principal at the high school was a little bit surprised at me running," she said. "He wasn't sure he wanted me to run in meets. I mean a lot of people frowned on women's sports."[1] No sooner had she returned in September than the administration presented her with a silver loving cup in honor of her achievement.

The exhibition at Thornton was one of several she ran for a variety of organizations in local communities. She also served as celebrity official at a number of swimming and skating meets and spoke at banquets throughout the area. Somehow Robinson thrived on such a hectic schedule, although it severely tested her time management skills. Among the list of "things I can't remember" by Don Mackenzie, the editor in chief of the yearbook, was "Babe Robinson being on time."

In the midst of all the hubbub, the senior changed her goals for the second time since she entered high school. On the first occasion, she decided to forgo dancing and consider a career as a Latin teacher after studying the subject and spending two years in the Latin club. But her overnight success in track and her subsequent exposure to some of the renowned coaches in the sport led her to imagine a life as a physical education instructor. In her yearbook profile, under the category of ambition, she wrote: "To be a coach of the 1936 American Olympic Team."

At the time, of course, she had other prospects for 1932, when she would be only 20 years old. Her plan was to defend her 100-meter title in Los Angeles, after which she would be free to coach others, thus becoming a "professional" in the eyes of Olympic officials and no longer eligible to compete.

"There was no real thought of money at that stage," she recalled. "I could have endorsed something after winning in 1928 but my father said, 'Absolutely not, because if you do that you can't compete anymore, and you've just started.' So I never did endorse any product."[2]

Instead, Betty Robinson became a personification of the amateur ideal as envisioned by Pierre de Coubertin, Douglas MacArthur, and Avery Brundage. She was held up as a role model by her elders, admired by her peers, and idolized by younger girls whom she encouraged to compete.

"She was beautiful, friendly and very competitive," said Ed Kipley, an athlete who grew up on East 137th Street in the house behind Robinson's three-flat and occasionally trained with her during her final year of high school. "Some of the neighbors thought she was a tomboy, but nobody ever said that to her face."[3]

For Betty, competition wasn't limited to the track. That became clear when she was elected to the National Honor Society at Thornton, where her average of 4.937 on a scale of 5.0 ranked her among the top ten in her class.

Temporarily freed from her studies, she intensified her preparation for the 1929 national AAU championships, staged for the first time in Chicago, on July 27. In a field that included ten of her teammates from Amsterdam, she proved her Olympic success was no fluke. This time she entered the 50-yard dash as well as the 100-yard dash. (Since it wasn't an Olympic year the metric sprint distances were discontinued.) Not only did she win both events but she smashed world records in both.

They were among five records bettered in the course of the afternoon at Soldier Field. Helen Filkey, returning to competition after her disappointment in the 1928 Olympic trials and a subsequent marriage, lowered the mark in the 80-meter hurdles to 12⅗ seconds. Rena McDonald, an Olympian the previous year, tossed the shot put 42 feet, 4½ inches, and Gloria Russell of California threw a baseball 258 feet and 1 inch.

But it was Robinson who electrified the meet. According to the *Chicago Tribune* story on July 28, "The slim, smiling Chicago girl who runs like a man clipped one-fifth of a second off her own 50-yard dash mark, sprinting the distance in 5⅘ seconds. In the longer dash she broke the accepted mark of 11⅖ seconds, held jointly by herself and Helen Filkey Warren, a clubmate, in the semi-final heat by one-fifth of a second and equaled the performance in the final."

Loretta McNeil and Jessie Cross, two Olympic teammates from New York's Millrose Athletic Association, were second in the respective races, but neither offered a strong challenge. Millrose coach Mel Sheppard, who had overseen the U.S. women's team at Amsterdam, marveled at the progress Robinson had made in the last year. "I never thought I'd live to see the day," he said, "when a girl could run like that."[4]

One month shy of her 18th birthday, Babe Robinson indisputably reigned as the world's fastest female.

Yet, a serious threat was emerging to the east. Her name was Stanisława Walasiewicz. Born in April 1911, in Poland, she accompanied her parents to the United States while an infant. The family settled in Cleveland, where, in true American fashion, she shortened her name to Stella Walsh. On May 30, 1930, she became the first woman to break the 11-second barrier for 100 yards.

Although she had failed to qualify for the final of the 100 meters in the 1928 Olympic trials, Walsh had made great strides thereafter. She enjoyed an outstanding indoor season in early 1930, defeating Myrtle Cook and two other Canadian speedsters in the 50-yard dash at the Millrose Games in Madison Square Garden and winning the 220 at the national AAU indoor championships at Boston Garden.

Unlike the fair, five-foot-six Robinson, Walsh was broad-shouldered, with muscular legs and a dark complexion. She augmented the speed to run the sprints with the athleticism to compete in the broad jump and the strength to throw the discus. She also projected a sense of mystery, arriving at meets in her running clothes, never changing in the locker room, and leaving immediately after a meet ended.

Walsh was a file clerk in the Cleveland office of the New York Central Railroad, and her stunning 10.8 second time in the 100-yard dash led to the nickname of "Cleveland's 20th Century Limited." She also was accorded numeral 1 in the list of entries at the 1930 national AAU championships. She lived up to the former and the latter in a brilliant performance at Southern Methodist University in Dallas, dethroning Robinson in a thrilling 100-yard race before easily winning the 220-yard dash and defeating Texas youngster Mildred Didrikson in the broad jump.

"In the 100-yard dash," Louise Mead Tricard later wrote, "Stella was pressed from the gun to the tape by Betty Robinson. Both women ran stride for stride for the distance, and inches separated them at the finish."[5]

So close were they that both runners were timed in 11.2 seconds and Robinson's supporters argued for a dead heat. But Walsh carried away the honors and shortly thereafter sailed for Europe to participate in the third Women's World Championships at Prague, at the invitation of her native country. (The United States did not send a team.) According to the *Amateur Athlete,* Walsh, representing Poland, won "the 80, 100 and 200 meter championships of the world" and returned home to a rousing reception in New York and Cleveland.

Meanwhile, Robinson had begun a new phase of her life. After taking courses at Thornton Junior College, she transferred her credits to Northwestern University on the lakefront north of Chicago and plunged into student life on the Big Ten campus. She pledged to the Kappa Kappa Gamma sorority and joined the women's rifle team. Of course, track remained her paramount extracurricular activity and she gained a knowledgeable and widely respected coach in Frank Hill. His primary job was to work with the men's team, but he willingly added Robinson to his stable of runners.

"Betty has a lot of natural ability," he told the *Chicago Tribune,* "but never has trained hard. She has several years of running ahead of her, and I believe that when she goes into hard training there will be few who will offer her any serious competition. She is fast, responds to instruction and is tending to her schooling and training."[6]

Robinson had seriously considered matriculating at the University of Illinois, where Charles Price had earned his bachelor's degree. "Now I am so glad that I came to Northwestern," she said. "The instructors are just wonderful, especially Mr. Hill. He has been giving me a lot of valuable advice about training and running. The modern equipment is making play out of this physical education course, which I thought at first would be difficult."[7]

At Evanston, she found a comfortable balance between class work and training. "I always have been active," she said, "and after a workout on the track I feel all pepped up for my studies. I enjoy it tremendously. The routine of studying would be dull if I did not have some outside interest."[8]

It wasn't long before Betty's outside interests included Bert Riel. While adhering to Hill's training rules of no smoking, no drinking, and no staying out late, she became attracted to the three-sport letterman, a big man on campus. He was similarly smitten.

In addition to being a star singles player for the Northwestern tennis team and a reserve halfback and placekicker for the foot-ball team, "Ball Hawk" Riel was the captain of the most success-ful basketball team in school history. The Wildcats won sixteen of seventeen games and earned their first and only undisputed Big Ten championship in the 1930–31 season. The two athletes had a lot in common, not the least of which was their public prominence.

The relationship added another layer of confidence to Robinson's armor as she approached her rivalry with Walsh. Officials of the Il-linois Women's Athletic Club had been trying to arrange a rematch with the Polish-American sprinter ever since the breathtaking finish at the AAU championships the previous summer, and they finally managed to secure a so-called "match race" for February 23, 1931, at the 24th Field Artillery Armory on the South Side of Chicago. To provide additional prestige to the race, staged as the centerpiece of the Illinois National Guard and Naval Militia track meet, an invita-tion also was sent to Myrtle Cook, who had anchored Canada's 4 × 100-meter relay victory in the Olympic Games and shared the unof-ficial world record at 100 meters with Robinson.

When Cook was felled by an illness, she was replaced by Evelyne Hall, a rising hurdler with Robinson's club. In truth, there was no need for a third party in the race, which was the first ever held for women on a 100-yard indoor straightaway. Both champions battled evenly through the first 95 yards before Robinson appeared to lunge ahead in the final strides. Observers judged her margin over Walsh to be a foot or less. Hall was a distant third. The winning time was 11.1 seconds.

Buoyed by that performance, which earned her a miniature track shoe with a diamond from her club, Betty entered the 60-yard dash in the Central AAU indoor meet at the Oak Park High School field house the following month. Among a field that included Ralph Met-calfe, the sensational freshman sprinter from Marquette University, and Lee Sentman, the NCAA champion hurdler from the Univer-sity of Illinois, the Northwestern undergraduate stole the show once more.

Rocketing down the track and pulling away from Ethel Harrington and Hall, also representing the IWAC, Robinson established an indoor record of 6.9 seconds.

Under Hill's guidance, she also had been extending her workouts to prepare for longer races. The coach thought there was no reason she couldn't be just as successful at 220 yards (and 200 meters) as at 100 yards and 100 meters. In June, at a meet in Milwaukee, she demonstrated the wisdom of his counsel when she broke the record for the 220 with a clocking of 25.1 seconds.

In a double likely never to be duplicated, she was a finalist for the inaugural Sullivan Award honoring the best American amateur athlete (Grand Slam golf champion Bobby Jones was the winner) and a contestant in the Miss Chicago beauty pageant. Almost as remarkably, she led the Northwestern women's rifle team in points in her first year of competition and was elected captain for the following fall.

Socially, scholastically, and athletically, she was positioned to achieve all her goals, to reach for the highest honors and the greatest rewards. Before the month was out, Betty Robinson found herself back at the starting line, facing a more difficult set of opponents.

---

# Crash

From the top of the world to the bottom of a heap, the distance was several hundred feet. One minute Betty Robinson was airborne, with a future as dazzling as the view from her cousin's aircraft, the next minute she was plunging toward the earth and a grim prognosis. The resulting crash threatened her life and appeared to terminate her running career.

Eager to reclaim the title as the world's fastest woman, she was in the best shape of her life that morning as she had demonstrated at practice with members of the Illinois Women's Athletic Club. After defeating Stella Walsh in an indoor race in April, she was gearing up for a showdown at the 1931 AAU championships in Jersey City the following month. All she remembered about that day, Sunday, June 28, was that it was hot, so hot that she sought an escape from the stagnant air hovering over Chicago.

The pool at the club never looked so inviting. But coaches discouraged swimming as an exercise for runners because it involved different muscles. That left her with one recourse, a telephone call to her cousin. One year younger than Betty, Wilson Palmer had recently received a pilot's license and purchased, in conjunction with two partners, a Waco biplane. It had to be cooler up there among the clouds above Lake Michigan, Betty reasoned.

"Betty loved flying and did not know the meaning of fear," her sister, Mrs. Jean Rochfort, told the *Chicago Tribune*. "I believe she has been up before with Palmer and she has often been up in other planes and has been interested in flying for the last two years."[1]

Deciding to make a picnic of it, Betty picked up her mother and nephew in Riverdale and drove to the grass field on the outskirts of Harvey where Palmer kept his plane. His two partners had just finished a flight when Betty arrived. The Waco 10, popular among civilian pilots, was paired with an old Curtiss OX-5 engine, a design that was considered neither advanced nor powerful.

Wearing goggles, a leather helmet, and what one newspaper said were colorful beach pajamas, Betty climbed into the front seat and Palmer into the rear pilot's seat of the open cockpit. Palmer, the son of Mrs. Robinson's sister, Fanny, was employed as a messenger by the National Safety Company and lived around the corner from the Robinsons. Betty waved to her mother as the plane rumbled by, gaining sufficient speed for takeoff.

According to witnesses, the Waco had reached an altitude between 400 and 600 feet when the motor stalled. The plane nosedived, burying itself in the damp earth. All that prevented a complete calamity were the soft condition of the field and Palmer's presence of mind. He cut the ignition before impact, avoiding a potential fire.

Both bodies lay underneath the rubble when rescuers reached them. They were unconscious. Noting her broken left arm, mangled left leg, and eight-inch gash across her forehead, the man who pulled Robinson from the debris anticipated the worst. He placed the broken body in the trunk of his car and drove her, in Betty's words, to "an old people's home, because he had a friend there who was an undertaker, and he thought I was dying."[2]

Actually, Oak Forest was an infirmary to which the city of Chicago and Cook County sent their indigent patients. It was known locally as the "Poor Farm," and the majority of the elderly inhabitants were hospitalized for chronic care, mental illness, or tuberculosis. Robinson wasn't in imminent need of an undertaker but her condition was critical.

The physicians on duty administered X-rays, inserted silver pins in her damaged limb, and applied casts. "The thigh bone is fractured in several places between the knee and the hip and when it heals it will probably be a little shorter than the other leg," explained Dr. Jacob Minke. "It will be months before she is able to walk again. She has a fractured left arm and internal injuries which may be more serious than is yet apparent."[3]

While she was presumed dead only momentarily, the next day's newspapers painted a gloomy picture. Headlines ranged from "Girl Runner Will Never Race Again" to "Crash Will End Athletics For Betty Robinson" to "Thousands Hope Against Surgeons' Verdict that Betty Will Run No More." For melodramatic schlock value, nothing topped the lead from the *Evening American* of June 29: "Lying almost paralyzed on a cot, Betty Robinson today fought to win the hardest race she ever ran—a race in which the Grim Reaper was pacing her."

Palmer also was in critical condition after being rushed to Ingalls Memorial Hospital in Harvey. He also suffered several fractures and, after a quarter century of pain, would undergo the amputation of his left leg.

Although Robinson was declared out of danger two days after the crash, she drifted in and out of consciousness for some time. Of her hospital stay, she remembered almost nothing but lying in a bed with her arm and both legs encased in plaster. "I had a lapse of memory the whole summer," she said years later in a taped interview for the Bud Greenspan documentary.[4]

She didn't remember taking her mother and nephew to the field nor did she remember attending a big party the night before the crash.

Her father sounded the first notes of optimism. "Betty is getting along as well as her mother and I could wish," Harry Robinson said within days of the accident. "Her temperature is almost normal and she is resting easily. Her spine is not, as we feared, injured, and there are no symptoms of any serious internal injuries. If the broken bones in her arm and leg knit satisfactorily, there is some chance that Betty will run again. At least, that is what we are all hoping."[5]

It was a month before Betty was able to receive visitors other than her immediate family and Bert Riel. Even then, the faces came and went without acknowledgment. "I would say hello to people," she noted, "but after they left I didn't know they'd been there. The convalescence went on for a very long time. . . . But I was lucky. The doctor said if I hadn't been in such good condition I wouldn't have come out of it as well as I did."[6]

She was finally able to leave Oak Forest on September 6, exactly eleven weeks after the accident, and the casts weren't removed from her legs until the end of September, allowing her to transfer from a bed to a wheelchair.

While she was hospitalized, New Jersey native Eleanor Egg upset Stella Walsh at 100 yards in the national championships in Jersey City, although her winning time, 11.4, was well off the American record of 11.2 established by Robinson in 1929 and equaled by Walsh in 1930. Walsh did win the 220 but Robinson had consistently been beating her time of 26.4 in practice before that fateful June afternoon.

"Betty never had a chance to run her best race," said Frank Hill, the Northwestern coach. "If it hadn't been for the accident, she would have far exceeded all her previous efforts and would have set marks in the 100- and 220-yard runs. This would have placed her far ahead of all contenders."[7]

Instead, in Robinson's absence, another Babe assumed the mantle of America's most celebrated female track star. Mildred (Babe) Didrikson, a lean 19-year-old from Beaumont, Texas, staked her claim to greatness at Pershing Field on July 25 by winning all three events in which she was entered. She followed a world record performance of 12 seconds flat in the 80-yard hurdles by finishing first in the running broad jump and the baseball throw, a peculiarly American event that remained on the AAU program through 1957.

The hurdles race was of particular interest because it had been added to the Olympic program for 1932. That should have been good news for Helen Filkey, Robinson's star-crossed friend from the IWAC. The perennial champion had fallen in the 1930 nationals at

Dallas and lost for the first time in six years, but demonstrated her fitness by finishing first in the 1931 Central AAU meet one week before Jersey City.

It would prove to be the final amateur competition of her life. Because she had taken a job for a company that prepared trophies and medals for athletic meets, and thus was perceived to be in a position to benefit financially from her prowess, Filkey was declared a professional by the AAU. She never got the opportunity to challenge Didrikson, and her Olympic dreams were terminated.

Meanwhile, with the help of Riel and family members who had to carry her wheelchair up and down the stairs from her second-floor apartment, Robinson was able to begin her rehabilitation. From there she graduated to crutches and, not long before Christmas, she was back on her feet. After months in a cast, the act of walking was a chore.

Yet, not for a minute did Robinson consider retirement.

"Of course, I am going to try to run again," Betty told the *Chicago Tribune*. "After spending the last eight years in preparation for an athletic career, it would be useless for me to give up without at least an attempt to run. But just when I will be able to begin strenuous training is up to the doctors. In the meantime I am going to continue my course in physical education at Northwestern. . . ."

"Not being able to race is terrible to contemplate, but I have determined not to let this accident ruin my life."[8]

She started slowly, jogging to Riverdale Park and back. Soon she enlisted the more athletic of her brothers-in-law, Jim Rochfort, to pace her. She would give him a half-block lead and try to catch him before he reached the park. To Rochfort and the neighbors who witnessed the efforts, the metal in her leg made the sound of firecrackers on the Fourth of July.

Returning to campus, she placed herself in the capable hands of Hill and Northwestern's training staff. "The coaches at Northwestern have promised to do everything within their power to get me in running condition," Robinson said. "The doctors said that with massage the stiffness in my knee and elbow would disappear. Racing starts have always been difficult for me, and a stiff left arm would be too great a handicap to overcome. I walk with a barely perceptible limp now, which is rapidly disappearing."[9]

Mindful of the U.S. Olympic trials that, in a pleasant coincidence, were scheduled to be held at Northwestern in mid-July, she made it to the track at Dyche Stadium in April. After a few weeks of light training, she filled out entry forms for the 50- and 100-yard dash events at the 1932 Central AAU championships at Ogden Park in June. But as willing as was her spirit, she lacked the conditioning for such an endeavor. And the lack of flexibility in her knee made it impossible to settle into a sprinter's crouch at the start.

On the advice of her coach and doctors, and with great reluctance, Robinson conceded the 1932 Games would have to go on without her. The entry list for the 1932 AAU championships and Olympic trials would include twelve of the nineteen Americans who participated in Amsterdam.

The competitors included the first three runners in the 4 × 100-meter relay team that earned the silver medal—Mary Washburn, Jessie Cross, and Loretta McNeil, from New York. Lillian Copeland, who finished second in the discus, as well as Maybelle Reichardt and sprinter Anne Vrana from Los Angeles, returned for another attempt at Olympic glory. So did Jean Shiley, the high jumper from Philadelphia who just missed a medal in 1928; Robinson's former cabinmates from St. Louis, Dee Boeckmann and Catherine Maguire; as well as discus and javelin thrower Margaret Jenkins from San Francisco; and discus thrower Rena MacDonald and sprinter Olive Hasenfus from Boston.

Among the missing were Elta Cartwright, the individual star of the Olympic trials in Newark, who had become a full-time teacher in Northern California. The demise of the 800 meters spelled an end to the competitive careers of Florence McDonald and Rayma Wilson. Mildred Wiley, third in the high jump at Amsterdam, was 30 years old, married, and had started a family that would include a future professional football star, Bob Dee, the following year. Marion Holley, another high jumper, and reserve sprinter Edna Sayer retired from athletics after the 1928 Olympics.

And, of course, the field at Evanston did not include Babe Robinson, although she was very much present. In fact, at the request of organizers, she served as an official for the meet that became a star vehicle for Babe Didrikson, beginning with the opening parade of athletes where she appeared as the entire team representing the Employers Casualty Company of Dallas. Since organizers had placed no restrictions as to how many of the events in which she could enter, Didrikson decided upon eight.

"For two and a half hours," Didrikson said, "I was flying all over the place. I'd run a heat in the 80 meter hurdles and then I'd take one of my high jumps. Then I'd go over to the broad jump and take a turn at that. Then they'd be calling me for the javelin or the eight-pound shot."[10] Time constraints prevented her from tackling the 50-yard dash and the 100-meter run. She also had to decline a spot in the 4 × 100-meter relay for the lack of teammates. Otherwise, she kept herself busy, and opponents in some events waiting, as she waded through the afternoon. By the time she had finished, Didrikson had won the national AAU championships all by herself.

The Texan won five events and tied for first in a sixth. She finished fourth in the discus and failed to place only in the 220-yard dash. Her multiple successes enabled Employers Casualty to claim the team title with 30 points, eight more than were awarded the 22-member home team from the Illinois Women's Athletic Club.

Thanks to her "one-woman team" performance, Didrikson became an overnight sensation. And by winning the 80-meter hurdles and javelin throw, two events added to the Olympic program in Los Angeles, as well as tying Shiley for first in the high jump, she stamped herself as the person of greatest interest as well as the woman to beat in California. As Olympic historian David Wallechinsky later wrote:

> Olympic rules limited Babe to only three events, even
> though she had qualified for five, so she chose the three at
> which she had set world records. On the train across the
> country to the Los Angeles Olympics, Babe irritated her
> fellow teammates by playing the harmonica, exercising in
> the aisles and bragging about her numerous feats, which in-

cluded a blue ribbon for sewing at the Texas State Fair. The same qualities that annoyed athletes delighted reporters. Upon arrival in California, she told them, "I am out to beat everybody in sight and that's just what I'm going to do."[11]

The team that entrained from Chicago featured three veterans of the 1928 Olympics—Shiley, Copeland, and Jenkins—as well as the first two African American Olympians, sprinters Tidye Pickett from Chicago and Louise Stokes from Massachusetts. But from the first day of competition, when Didrikson won the javelin with a world record toss on her initial throw, the spotlight belonged to the brash Texan. She also finished first in controversial fashion in the 80-meter hurdles, defeating Evelyne Hall of the IWAC by inches, if at all. Both women were clocked in 11.7 seconds, a world record.

Finally, Didrikson was enmeshed in another controversy as she battled Shiley for the gold medal in the high jump. Both women cleared the world record height of 5 feet, 5¼ inches, but neither was able to top 5'6". Although both succeeded in a subsequent jump-off, Didrikson's Western roll caused her head to cross the bar before her body, a style known as "diving" and disallowed among women at the time. She was disqualified and Shiley was declared the winner.

Copeland won a fourth gold medal for the United States in her final toss of the discus, establishing another world record, and the American relay team of Mary Carew, Evelyn Furtsch, Annette Rogers, and Wilhelmina von Bremen nosed out the Canadians, who also boasted four first timers, in the 4 × 100-meter relay. Remarkably, the United States won all the women's track and field events in Los Angeles except the one in which it triumphed in Amsterdam.

With Robinson back in Chicago, Stella Walsh was the prohibitive favorite to win the 100-meter dash and she disappointed only the American officials, who were expecting her to compete for the United States.

"As a result of the worldwide depression, she lost her job with the New York Central Railroad," Wallechinsky wrote. "She was offered a position with the Cleveland Recreation Department, but taking it would have made her ineligible for the Olympics, since Olympic regulations at the time disqualified athletes who made their living from physical education or recreation. With no help coming from her adopted country, Stella Walsh made a major decision in her life. Twenty-four hours before she was scheduled to take out U.S. naturalization papers, she accepted a job offer from the Polish consulate in New York and decided to compete for Poland."[12]

Wearing the red and white colors of Poland, she equaled the world record of 11.9 seconds in each of her three races in Los Angeles. Walsh was pressed by Canadian Hilde Strike in the final, but she surged from behind to win by half a yard. Von Bremen, the top American sprinter, finished another foot back in third place.

Whether Robinson would have beaten Walsh was the subject for a sleepless night. But by the time the Los Angeles Olympics had concluded, Betty Robinson was more concerned with starting a new chapter in her life.

Wedding photograph of Betty's parents, Harry and Elizabeth (Wilson)
Robinson

Dance was Betty's first love.

A three-time gold medalist in the 1924 Olympic Games, Johnny Weissmuller posed for pictures with many of the Olympic athletes en route to Amsterdam in 1928. Here he is with Betty, his fellow Chicagoan, whom he promised to chaperone.

A group of the 1928 U.S. women's track and field team in the dining room of the SS *President Roosevelt*. Betty is seated at far right in front of the waiter.

The lone American in the women's 100-meter final at the 1928 Summer Games, Betty Robinson won the gold medal and set a world's record, finishing just ahead of Canadian favorite Fanny Rosenfeld (*left*).

In Chicago, just a few days after her 17th birthday, a triumphant Betty, accompanied by her parents, accepts an award for her Olympic performance.

Page One Hundred Thirty-five

Betty "Babe" Robinson, in her high school yearbook, *The Thortonite*, 1929

Officially the world's fastest female runner, Betty electrified the national AAU championships at Soldier Field in Chicago on July 27, 1929, with a pair of world records.

As a student at Northwestern University, Betty was a contestant in the Miss Chicago beauty pageant.

When the SS *Manhattan* cast off for Hamburg from Pier 60 in New York Harbor on the morning of July 15, 1936, there were nine first timers among the women, including prospective star Helen Stephens. Athletes had to scramble for funds to participate. With mere hours to go before the ship sailed, the American Olympic Committee announced that the full delegation of 382 athletes would be sent to Berlin.

Members of the 1936 U.S. Olympic women's track and field team aboard the SS *Manhattan*. Helen Stephens is top left with fellow relay contestants Annette Rogers just below her, Harriet Bland far left, and Betty second from the right in the bottom row.

After many days of travel with little exercise, the Americans needed workouts to regain their competitive edge. They had about a week to recuperate, and Betty (as well as Helen Stephens, Kathlyn Kelly, and Dee Boeckmann) also found time for shopping in Berlin.

The celebrated airship *Hindenburg,* with a Nazi swastika on its tail fin, floats above the Olympic Stadium before the opening ceremony in Berlin on August 1, 1936, launching the most controversial, most politicized, most grandiose, and most efficient Olympics in history.

The women's track and field team was a cheerful group compared with some of their fellow Olympians. New York mustered enough excitement to stage its first ticker-tape celebration in three years. Helen Stephens (*top left*) and Betty Robinson (*top right*), along with several other female athletes and coach Dee Boeckmann, shared the second automobile in the parade, behind the one carrying Jesse Owens.

### A Typical American Girl

*A Typical American Girl, in my opinion,
should possess the following qualifications:*

1. *Willingness to cooperate with others.*
2. *Willingness to accept responsibility.*
3. *Initiative.*
4. *Good sportsmanship.*
5. *Courage.*
6. *At least one accomplishment.*
7. *Health.*

*Beauty of feature is not included because a
girl has beauty if she possesses a good healthy
personal appearance as a whole.*

*Betty Robinson
Olympics - 1928-1936.*

"A Typical American Girl"

*Top:* Dick and Betty Schwartz just before their wedding, which was held on December 1, 1939, in a private service at the parsonage of the First Methodist Church of Dolton, a few blocks from Betty's Riverdale home (Associated Press photo). *Bottom:* Betty with son, Rick (b. 1942), and daughter, Jane (b. 1946).

Cereal box card, 1954

Betty again became a person of interest at the approach of the 1996 Olympics in Atlanta. Prior to releasing a card set of Olympic legends, including Robinson, the Upper Deck company invited Betty and her husband to a promotion in Santa Monica, California. Betty is shown with Bob Mathias, Florence Griffith-Joyner (her eventual successor as the fastest female on the planet), Nadia Comaneci, and Muhammad Ali. Gymnastics coach Béla Károlyi and 1996 Olympian Dominique Moceanu are also pictured.

# CHAPTER 11

# Down and Out

She was not unlike millions of other Americans who had been buffeted by forces beyond their control in the summer of 1932. Although her injuries had been largely external, Betty Robinson shared the experience of shattered dreams with many whose very existence had been reduced by the ravages of the Great Depression.

As the Los Angeles Olympics went on without her and she faced the continuing costs and trauma of rehabilitation, she reluctantly left behind the life of Betty Coed. Unable to stand for long periods of time, she acknowledged, "I couldn't participate in practice teaching, which I had to do for my degree. So I decided to become a secretary."[1]

At least she had a job, at a commercial art company in the Loop. But the relationship with Bert Riel frayed and tattered.

There were changes everywhere. Even the Illinois Women's Athletic Club, which had supported Betty from the moment she finished her first competition, was feeling the pinch. It would disband within the year.

Meanwhile, Harry Robinson had been told to reduce the wages of the employees under his supervision. He declined, asking his superiors to cut his salary instead. A standoff ensued and he left his job to become the director of security at the nearby Acme Steel plant.

Betty's sister Evelyn Mills, recently widowed, opened a hair salon in the front room of her first-floor apartment. It was a time to make do.

Betty Robinson's connection to track was limited to speeches before school assemblies, service clubs, and civics groups promoting the benefits to health and citizenship from athletic competition among women. For the first time in her life, she was a spectator, not a participant. She did jog, if only to ease the stiffness in her left leg and promote a full recovery, but with a slight limp.

After a year and a half of routine inactivity, she began to consider a comeback. She reconnected with her former teammates on the IWAC, who now were training under the banner of the Lincoln Park Athletic Association. Still not in condition to run an individual race, she volunteered for the 4 × 100-meter relay at the 1934 national AAU indoor championships in Brooklyn on April 14.

"She did not win a prize of any sort and her racing was hardly noticed in the excitement of the relay," noted track journalist Jesse Abramson in the May edition of *Amateur Athlete*. That's because the relay team, with Robinson running the third leg, finished a desultory fourth in the competition. The meet was dominated by Stella Walsh, who won both the 50-meter and 200-meter races. Walsh won the latter in world-record time, defeating Annette Rogers from the Lincoln Park team by a full 12 yards.

Abramson reported that Robinson had been training for a month before the meet, her first in almost three years. "Although she ran only in the relay," he said, "she intends to compete in the outdoor nationals and hopes to go to London this summer for the women's world international meet and then make the 1936 Olympic team."

But the outdoor nationals were canceled, the United States did not send an official delegation to the women's world games (where Walsh was beaten by Käthe Krauss of Germany in both the 100 and 200 meters), and Robinson struggled with a pulled leg muscle. She did, however, benefit from additional training time and, in early August, helped her team to a relay victory in the Central AAU championships at Ogden Park in the respectable time of 49.6.

While Robinson was gearing up for the 1935 campaign, a talented newcomer emerged from virtual obscurity in much the way Betty had seven years earlier. Helen Stephens, a 17-year-old farm girl from Fulton, Missouri, made a sensational debut at the national AAU indoor championships in St. Louis.

Not only did she win three events but she overcame the experienced Walsh in the 50-meter dash. Stephens didn't even own a tracksuit or her own pair of spikes. Her high school coach, Burt Moore, paid the two-dollar entry fee and drove her the 110 miles to the new St. Louis Arena on Friday, March 22. But the teenager had what couldn't be taught or bought.

Standing almost six feet tall, Stephens had regularly raced her cousin, who was on horseback, the mile to the one-room schoolhouse she attended from the first through eighth grades. She had been sprinting for a finish line in her daydreams almost as long as she could remember. So, wearing a gym suit and spikes borrowed from members of the boys' track team, she walked to the starting line without fear after winning the shot put and the standing broad jump.

Running in her very first official race over the clay track, she beat local favorite Harriet Bland, a protégé of Dee Boeckmann, to the tape in 6.6 seconds, tying the American record. Facing the celebrated Walsh in the final, she jumped into the lead and widened it with each of her nine-foot strides. Stephens again was timed in 6.6 and there was at least a yard between her and the Olympic champion at the finish.

When an excited reporter asked her what she thought about beating the great Stella Walsh, she allegedly replied, "Who is Stella Walsh?" Although many thought it was evidence of her naïveté, the truth is Stephens had full knowledge of her opponent's reputation and, according to her biography, was practicing the dry wit she employed as the jokes editor for the Fulton High School newspaper. If nothing else, it did help to stimulate a rivalry between the athletic women who otherwise had so little in common.[2]

Stephens set a world record of 11.6 for the 100 meters in the Missouri Valley AAU championships at St. Louis in June and established unofficial records at various distances in exhibitions throughout the summer before and after her high school graduation. With the aid of Boeckmann, the former Olympian who was the AAU district chairperson and newly appointed coach of the Olympic women's team, Moore mapped out a schedule for Stephens culminating in Canada's National Exhibition for girls under 18 on August 31 and the AAU national outdoor championships in New York on September 14.

After tying the Canadian and world record of 10.8 seconds for 100 yards in Toronto, Stephens arrived in New York with a colorful backstory and great expectations she did nothing to dispel. Thrilling a small crowd on a chilly, threatening day at New York University's Ohio Field, she easily won both the 100 and 200 meters, equaling her own world record of 11.6 seconds in the former. As if to prove she was human, she finished second behind Margaret Wright in the discus by two feet, 2¾ inches. In the span of three hours, she accounted for 13 points, enabling Fulton High School, which did not field a women's track team, to finish fourth in the overall team score, although Stephens already had enrolled at William Woods College, a private institution for women located in her hometown. "Miss Stephens' performance was hailed on all sides by officials and spectators alike," stated an article in the *New York Times*. "Frederick W. Rubien, secretary of the Olympic committee, and Daniel F. Ferris, secretary of the AAU, frankly admitted that they consider this latest star a potential champion in the next Olympic Games. The winner, pressed at no time, obviously slackened her pace at the finish of the century, and experts who take into account her slight amount of coaching feel there is no telling how far she may eventually lower the records."[3]

The paper also stated that Stephens "combines the speed of Stella Walsh with the field versatility of Babe Didrikson." The latter's amateur career had concluded shortly after the Los Angeles Olympics, when she was barred by the AAU after her name and a photograph of her in mid-hurdle were used in an automobile advertisement. The fallout soured Brundage, the AAU president who had upheld women's right to compete in 1932, on the issue.

"You know," he told the *New York Times* on December 25 of that year, "the ancient Greeks kept women out of their athletic games. They wouldn't even let them on the sidelines. I'm not so sure but they were right."[4]

Not only did Stephens's rapid rise push Robinson's attempted comeback farther into the background, but it complicated her efforts to make the Olympic team. Clearly, the Missouri teenager would have been a handful for Robinson in her prime, but Betty was far from that in the summer of 1935. She did manage to win the 200 meters in the Central AAU meet in August, but her time, 26.6, was two seconds slower than the 24.6 managed by Stephens in New York. And Robinson finished third at Ogden Park in the 100 behind two other Chicagoans, Annette Rogers and Tidye Pickett.

Clearly, her chance to finish among the top three at the Olympic trials the following summer had been further compromised, and even a finish in the top six, which might warrant an opportunity to run in the 4 × 100 relay, would be a challenge. But Robinson wasn't about to curtail her comeback with the Olympics looming.

With her first full year of competition behind her, Stephens continued to amass records. For those who wondered about her room for improvement, the 1936 national AAU indoor meet served as a handy benchmark. For the second consecutive year, it was staged at the St. Louis Arena, with much of the same cast—minus Stella Walsh—from 1935.

"I believe Helen will better her record of 6.6 seconds in the 50 meters by two-tenths of a second if the track is good," Moore told the *St. Louis Post-Dispatch.* "She will also better her shot-put mark of 39 feet, 7¼ inches by two or three feet. She shouldn't have any trouble winning the broad jump at 8 feet, 6 inches. I kept her out of the 200 meters because she is recovering from a very severe cold and I do not wish to tax her strength."[5]

At 18 years of age, Stephens was as good as predicted. In pulling away from Harriet Bland, she ran 6.4 in the 50, tying the indoor world record. She put the shot 41 feet, 7 inches, and leaped 8 feet, 8 inches, in the standing broad jump, easily winning both those titles. This time the results were credited to William Woods College instead of Fulton High School.

After setting two Canadian records during a meet in Hamilton, Ontario, Stephens accepted an invitation to compete in an elite 50-meter event at the Central AAU indoor championships in Chicago. Others invited included Stella Walsh, who declined. "Tell her," Walsh reportedly told meet organizers, "I'll beat her in Berlin."

Robinson also chose not to contest the race, the short distance minimizing any chance she had of overcoming a standing start. Rogers, emerging as her primary American opponent and the 200-meter winner in St. Louis, accepted the part of willing foil. Once more, Stephens tied the world record of 6.4. Although she finished second in that race, Rogers won the regulation 50-meter dash in 6.7 and also the 200 meter in 29.4.

Completing an exhausting evening, Rogers ran the anchor leg for the winning relay team from the Illinois Catholic Women's Club, the latest incarnation of the Lincoln Park AA and IWAC. Playing to her strength, Robinson ran the third leg of the relay. For the record, Robinson was a Methodist.

Of course, the goal for all involved was to peak on July 4 at the stadium of Brown University, where the national AAU championships and Olympic trials were scheduled as part of the tri-centennial celebration of Providence, Rhode Island. On the eve of the event, the athletes were invited to tour the Rhode Island state house and meet with Governor Theodore Green, who provided a civics lesson that the fortunate few might observe in Germany.

"Some of you are going to a country where the principles of political equality and religious liberty established here in Rhode Island by Roger Williams are denied," the governor said. "But stand up for your American ideals there . . . proudly."[6]

If there were even a shred of doubt that Stephens would be first to write her ticket to Berlin, it was erased in the initial preliminary heat of the 100-meter race where she zoomed to a world-record time of 11.7. It bettered by three-tenths of a second the 12.0 attributed to Josephine Warren, the second fastest of the six heat winners. The defending champion relaxed in her semifinal heat, coasting to a clocking of 11.8, and then revved it up again in the final with a second 11.7, running away from all opponents.

Meanwhile, the real pressure was on Robinson. Needing to finish among the top three in her preliminary heat to advance, she tracked Warren to a second-place finish. The other heat winners included club mates Annette Rogers and Mary Terwilliger. With the knowledge that it could be the final race of her career, Robinson needed to finish second or better in the semifinal heat headlined by Harriet Bland, and once more she dogged the leader to the tape.

Her task in the eight-woman final was to run with enough speed and savvy to earn a spot in the relay, an event at which she was the most experienced in the competition. This Robinson accomplished, finishing fifth behind Stephens, Rogers, Bland, and Olive Hasenfus. Her time was identical to the 12.5 she ran in the final of the 1928 Olympic trials despite her inability to start from a crouch.

"I couldn't bend down," she recalled, "but I could run."[7]

"Miss Robinson's comeback is the most remarkable of all," the *New York Times* reported. "Winner of the dash in 1928, she was so badly hurt in a subsequent airplane crash that it was feared she never would walk again, much less run, yet today she had enough speed to place second in her heats and be close up in a well-bunched final."[8]

For good measure, she combined with Rogers, Terwilliger, and Ethel Harrington to win the 400-meter relay in the excellent time of 48 seconds flat, securing the team title for the Illinois Catholic Women's Club.

Rogers, who had followed Robinson to Northwestern, also won the high jump with a leap of 5 feet, 2½ inches. Because of the restrictive amateur rules of the time, the reigning Olympic champion and world-record holder was prohibited from competing in the trials. Only 24, Jean Shiley had her heart set on making a third Olympic team and traveled from Philadelphia to New York to seek the permission of Dan Ferris, secretary and treasurer of the AAU.

"He dismissed me just like that," Shiley said. "I was declared a professional because after the '32 Games I had taught swimming and had done some lifeguarding to earn some money. That's how it was then. Ferris said no, and that was that."[9]

Clearly, the fortunes of this American team were going to rest almost entirely on the shoulders of the 165-pound Stephens. After winning the 100, the 18-year-old spun the discus 121 feet, 6½ inches, to claim that title. She also triumphed in the shot put, a non-Olympic event. Anne Vrana O'Brien, a 1928 Olympian, captured the 80-meter hurdles in 12 seconds flat, and her fellow Californian Martha Worst succeeded in the javelin with a toss of 125 feet, ¼ inch.

While coach Dee Boeckmann's original intention was to select her team following the meet and accompany them to the Lincoln Hotel in New York, awaiting the sail to Germany on July 15, there was a slight change in plans after the American Olympic Committee announced a deficit of almost $150,000. Several teams were warned that they might be left behind if they were unable to raise sufficient funds for the voyage, and the women's track and field team was temporarily slashed from seventeen members to four because of the shortage.

Among the reasons for the financial plight was the continued burden of the Depression. The identity of the host nation also was a contributing factor. There had been strong support for boycotting Berlin because of the policies of the chancellor and his party, and it wasn't until December 1935 that the final obstacle to participation was lifted—barely two months before the start of the fourth Winter Games at Garmisch-Partenkirchen in the Bavarian Alps.

With so little time to raise money for the passage and board of American athletes, the committee responded with scare tactics. After a 10-hour meeting at the New York Athletic Club on July 5, it announced that only the boxing and modern pentathlon teams had raised sufficient money for their passage on the SS *Manhattan*. Although the teams ranked in the top three for importance—men's track and field, men's swimming, and women's swimming—were considered among those in jeopardy, they had yet to hold their final tryouts, which were their principal sources of revenue.

"Frankly, we expect a sellout," said chairman Bill Bingham of the men's track and field group, which scheduled its trials for New York's Randall's Island on Saturday and Sunday. "And then we will net more than our budget, with the surplus turned over to the general fund."[10]

While stating that "unless we get the money in the next 10 days we can't sail," AOC president Avery Brundage said it was inconceivable that "the American public would let the American team down."[11] He also said he planned a nationwide radio appeal from the pier on the date of departure if necessary.

The four women's track and field athletes cleared for transit were Helen Stephens, Annette Rogers, Anne Vrana O'Brien, and Tidye Pickett. Although no explanation was offered for the order of selection, this would provide the Americans with two entrants in the 100 meters, two in the 80-meter hurdles, one in the high jump, one in the discus, and enough personnel to stock a relay team. Dee Boeckmann's duties were expanded from coach to manager, coach, and chaperone.

The warning was heeded by all the affected athletes. According to the Associated Press, Boeckmann's ladies raised money "by selling Olympic badges in the New York streets, by dunning public officials and asking the aid of newspapers."[12] In the case of Bland, the *St. Louis Globe-Democrat* raised the $500 minimum required for the trip. Kathlyn Kelly, the 16-year-old who earned the final spot in high jumping, received sponsorship from the South Carolina legislature. Robinson's father had to guarantee her passage. Others borrowed what they could.

On the same day that the New York Athletic Club donated $5,000, to be spread among track and field, fencing, swimming, and rowing, the Metropolitan AAU contributed $1,300. The mayor of West New York, New Jersey, underwrote the expenses for a pair of gymnasts from that city. A New York heiress offered $1,000 to the general fund. And a child from Harlem mailed a letter to Gustavus Kirby, treasurer of the Olympic fund, that included 10 three-cent stamps and the instruction: "I heard you need money and I want Jesse Owens to be on the team. Please see that he gets this."

While Kirby called it "deplorable" that some athletes had to, in effect, pay their own way to compete, he said additional funds raised by the committee would be used to refund the money. Day by day, dollar by dollar, the list of approved athletes expanded. Women's track and field grew from 5 to 9, then to 14, and, finally, on July 14, to 16. Later that day the men's field hockey team, with 15 members, was added and, last but not least, the female swimmers met their quota, their ranks swelling from 10 to 18.

So with mere hours to go before the ship sailed, the AOC announced that the full delegation of 382 athletes would be sent to Berlin. What they were about to encounter was the most controversial, most politicized, most grandiose, and most efficient Olympics in history.

CHAPTER 12

# Heil Brundage!

Adolf Hitler's warped vision of world leadership did not include hosting the Olympic Games. He had demonstrated no interest in sports, either as participant or spectator. But after his National Socialist Party scored a stunning victory in the 1932 parliamentary elections and he was appointed chancellor of Germany by President Paul von Hindenburg in January 1933, his administration inherited the stewardship of the 1936 Olympics that had been pledged to Garmisch-Partenkirchen in the winter and Berlin in the summer.

Berlin had been the choice of the International Olympic Committee for the 1916 Games, which were canceled by World War I, in which Germany played such a major role that its national team was barred from competition until 1928. When the International Olympic Committee voted to try again in the late spring of 1931, it was viewed as a show of support for the country's democratic government in the wake of severe reparations that created tremendous economic hardship. Alas, the nature of the government became the problem when Hitler rose to power.

"This was a man who as late as 1932 had denounced the Olympic Games as a 'plot of Freemasons and Jews,'" wrote the historian David Clay Large. "The prospect of a Hitler-led Germany possibly hosting the next Olympic Games presented the young Olympic movement with its greatest crisis to date."

Although Hitler's appetite for conquest had yet to threaten the Sudetenland, Poland, and Scandinavia, the party's anti-Semitic pronouncements and measures alarmed Jewish communities throughout the world, particularly in the United States. "In the wake of the government-orchestrated boycott of Jewish businesses across Germany on April 1, 1933," Large wrote, "Jewish representatives in the United States began appealing to leaders of the American Olympic movement to raise the possibility of moving the 1936 Summer Games out of Berlin."[1]

But the leader of the American Olympic movement, Avery Brundage, was more suspicious of the Jewish protesters than he was of German authorities. The Chicago construction magnate had traveled on his own to Germany in 1934 in what he termed a fact-finding mission. It consisted of a six-day excursion with Nazi Party official and IOC member Karl Ritter von Halt, against whom he had competed in the 1912 Olympics at Stockholm. Halt not only picked the people to whom Brundage spoke but translated for him.

"As if to put his Nazi hosts at ease, Brundage let it be known that his own men's club in Chicago barred Jews," reported Large. "This policy, he added, was a product of the American belief in 'separate but equal treatment,' an approach he believed was consistent with Olympic ideals. . . . On his return to America he submitted a report to the AOC Executive Committee full of praise for the German effort to be inclusive in its Olympic sports program. He then told the press that German officials had given him their word 'that there will be no discrimination in Berlin against Jews. You can't ask for more than that and I think the guarantee will be fulfilled.'"[2]

With his report in hand, the AOC voted unanimously to accept the German invitation to send a team to the Berlin Games.

"[Brundage] said politics should not be a factor and that the IOC would extract promises from Hitler to adhere to the Olympic Creed against discrimination based on race or religion," noted author David Maraniss. "But beneath that argument ran a deep river of anti-

Semitism. In a September 27, 1935, letter to Carl Diem, chief organizer of the Berlin Games, Brundage complained of a 'renewed outburst from our Jewish friends' against the Berlin Olympics. He insisted that the boycott effort 'pushed by Jews' was based on irresponsible propaganda, and asked Diem for data showing 'Jews going about their business in Germany as far as sports [are] concerned.'"[3]

Remarkably, this came in the aftermath of the Nuremberg Laws, which officially reclassified Jewish citizens as "subjects," depriving them of political rights and prohibiting them from marrying or even sleeping with Aryans. And while politically connected Jews may have spread the first seeds of a boycott, the movement had gathered steam among labor unions and Catholic groups.

Among the major speakers at an anti-Nazi rally at Madison Square Garden in June 1934 were Senator Millard Tydings of Maryland, former governor Al Smith of New York, New York City mayor Fiorello LaGuardia, and, surprisingly, Gustavus Kirby of the American Olympic Committee, who criticized Germany's attempts to deny Jewish athletes training facilities and the opportunity to earn places on the German Olympic team.

To counter the growing boycott movement in the United States, IOC president Baillet-Latour appealed to its three American members to "convince your people that the IOC has upheld the rights of everyone concerned and the unanimous decision [to keep the games in Berlin] was the only wise one."[4]

William May Garland, Charles Sherrill, and Ernest Jahncke had previously been contacted by the American Jewish Congress, which called upon the men "to take a firm stand against America's participation under the existing circumstances and conditions."[5]

Garland, a Los Angeles real estate mogul whose involvement with the IOC traced back to the 1932 Olympics in his city, sided with Baillet-Latour and Brundage in the belief there was no place in sports for politics, and that what Germany did to its own citizens was no business of the Olympics. Charles Sherrill, an accomplished sprinter while at Yale and a former U.S. ambassador to Turkey and Argentina, took a more aggressive approach to the problem.

"Sherrill traveled to Germany just prior to the 1935 Nuremberg Party Rally with the hope of persuading the Reich authorities to name at least one Jew to the German Olympic squads for 1936—a kind of athletic fig leaf," Large wrote. "On August 24 he discussed the matter personally with Hitler in Munich, proposing that Germany add a Jewish athlete to its team for the Berlin games, a symbolic gesture he compared with the American tradition of 'the token Negro.' He warned that if Germany did not do this, America might boycott Berlin."[6]

When Hitler rejected the plan outright, Sherrill discussed his proposal with Hans von Tschammer und Osten, the Reich sports leader. The person he had in mind was Gretel Bergmann, an outstanding high jumper whose plight of being removed from her sports club and forbidden from participating in the 1935 German track and field championships was well documented in the United States.

German officials did invite Bergmann back from England and named her to the German Olympic training team, enabling her to compete in qualifying meets. Although she won one event with a jump of 1.60 meters (5 feet, 3 inches), she was denied entry to the German championships from which the Olympic team was selected because of "inadequate qualifying performance."[7] The winning height in the women's Olympic high jump was 1.62 meters, achieved on a jump-off after a three-way tie for first at 1.60.

Sherrill's alternate for the role of "token" was Helene Mayer, who won a gold medal in fencing for Germany in 1928 and finished fifth in the 1932 Games at Los Angeles, where she remained as a student and then teacher. Although her father was Jewish, Mayer's mother was "Aryan," and so she was still considered a German citizen under the Nuremberg Laws. She also was eager to represent the new Germany and did not subscribe to the Jewish faith.

As an "honorary Aryan," she accepted an invitation to return and, indeed, was added to the German team. The host nation later added a half-Jewish hockey player named Rudi Ball, who had been living in Switzerland after leading Germany to a bronze medal at Lake Placid in 1932, on the last day for filing team rosters for the Winter Games.

"Sherrill returned to the United States convinced that with the Mayer concession he had dealt a fatal blow to the boycott movement," Large noted. "'I went to Germany,' he announced at a press conference, 'for the purpose of getting at least one Jew on the German Olympic team and I feel that my job is finished. As to obstacles placed in the way of Jewish athletes or any others in trying to reach Olympic ability, I would have no more business discussing that in Germany than if the Germans attempted to discuss the Negro situation in the American south or the treatment of Japanese in California."[8]

The third American IOC member, however, was of a different mind. Jahncke, a New Orleans shipbuilder with experience in rowing and yachting, was appalled by the Nuremberg Laws and subsequent reports of racial discrimination against Jewish athletes. Far from offering support to the IOC president, he wrote a scathing letter of condemnation.

"'The plain and undeniable fact is that the Nazis have consistently and persistently violated their pledges. Of this they have been convicted out of their own mouths and by the testimony of impartial and experienced American and English newspaper correspondents. . . . It is plainly your duty to hold the Nazi sports authorities accountable for the violation of their pledges. . . . I do not doubt that you have received all sorts of assurances from the Nazi sports authorities. Ever since they gave us their pledges in June, 1933, they have been lavish with their promises. The difficulty is that they have been stingy with their performance of them."[9]

"Judging from Baillet-Latour's correspondence files in the IOC archives, Jahncke's letter was probably the least reverential missive the Belgian aristocrat ever received," Large wrote. "Citing Baillet-Latour's invoking of the 'Olympic idea,' Jahncke said it was 'precisely [his] devotion to the Olympic idea' that caused him 'to do just the opposite of what you so confidently ask of me.' He would, he said, 'do all I can to persuade my fellow Americans that they ought not to take part in the Games if they are held in Nazi Germany.' Arguing that the Nazis had 'violated and are continuing to violate every requirement of fair play in the conduct of sports,' he insisted that no foreign nation could participate in the Nazi games 'without at least acquiescing in the contempt of the Nazis for fair play and their sordid exploitation of the Games.'"[10]

Jahncke, who had missed many IOC meetings in his service as assistant secretary of the navy under President Herbert Hoover, also offered a personal rebuke of Baillet-Latour. The latter responded in kind, citing the American's "willful ignorance" of the issues and concluding that "nothing but your resignation can be expected."[11]

For the IOC, however, Jahncke represented more of an internal problem. Emerging as the major impediment to the status quo was Jeremiah T. Mahoney, a strong-willed judge of the New York State Supreme Court and, as of 1935, the president of the Amateur Athletic Union. Mahoney and Brundage were good friends but they differed greatly on the issue of America's participation in the Berlin Olympics.

"Mahoney possessed an especially heightened sense of moral virtue or rectitude that influenced his life and work," wrote the Olympic historian John A. Lucas. "Such moral consciousness was irreconcilable with Brundage's pragmatism and unwavering support of his nation's Olympic Committee. Mahoney's passionate opposition to U.S. competition in the 1936 Olympic Games, while not unique among American AAU and USOC leaders, was of Olympian proportions, unrivaled by fellow Americans."[12]

Not only did Mahoney, a compelling public speaker, voice his opinion at every opportunity, he wrote an "open letter" to Theodor Lewald, the titular head of the German Organizing Committee but a man whose background—his father came from a prominent Jewish family that converted to Protestantism—was scorned by leaders of the Third Reich. In the letter, which consisted of thirteen typed pages, some of which he shared with the public, he accused Germany of "monstrous incidents of racism, brutality and genocide."

"It is contrary," he wrote, "to the fundamental motive behind the Olympic Games that they be held in a country where the spirit of decency and fair play has been so flagrantly violated."[13]

"The letter took on a painful personal note," Large noted, "when

Mahoney told Lewald that he feared the 'non-Aryan' official lacked 'any real authority' and was shamefully allowing himself to be 'used as a screen to conceal your government's flagrant violations of the Olympic ideal of fair play.' He called on Lewald to resign immediately from the GOC and the IOC."[14]

He also petitioned Baillet-Latour to move the Olympic Games from Berlin or face the prospect of an American boycott.

The IOC president did not respond directly to Mahoney. Instead, he urged Brundage to go on the offensive. The result was the publication of "Fair Play for American Athletes," a pamphlet distributed by the AOC to thousands of sports and civic groups. In *Nazi Games,* David Clay Large criticizes "Fair Play" extensively:

> In "Fair Play," Brundage set the tone with the opening statement, which smeared boycott advocates with a wide red brush: "In 1932 there was a concerted effort by Communists both here and abroad to wreck the Los Angeles Games. Many of the individuals and organizations active in the present campaign to boycott the Olympics have Communist antecedents. Radicals and Communists must keep their hands off American sport."
>
> Asking, "Shall the American athlete be made a martyr to a cause not his own?" the pamphlet pounded home the message that the boycott effort was alien and un-American, little short of treason. It also carried a warning to Jewish opponents of the German games: "Certain Jews had better understand that they cannot use these Games as a weapon in their boycott against the Nazis." Additionally, "Fair Play" advised the U.S. government not to interfere with the right of American athletes to go to Germany: "Will any of our athletes thank leaders who lose their heads in an argument having nothing to do with athletics and deny them the privilege of striving to maintain unbroken [the] tradition of American supremacy in world sport?"[15]

Brundage didn't have to worry about government interference. Despite protestations by American diplomats who had served in Germany after the Nazis came to power, the State Department offered no advice to the AOC or the AAU. And, whatever his misgivings, President Franklin D. Roosevelt maintained silence on the issue.

The president, according to the United States Holocaust Memorial Museum, "did not become involved in the boycott issue, despite warnings from high-level American diplomats regarding Nazi exploitation of the Olympics for propaganda purposes. Roosevelt continued a forty-year tradition in which the American Olympic Committee operated independently of outside influence. Both the U.S. ambassador to Germany, William E. Dodd, and George Messersmith, head of the U.S. delegation in Vienna, deplored the American Olympic Committee's decision to go to Berlin."[16]

The endgame occurred in December 1935 at the AAU convention in New York's Commodore Hotel. The AAU had the power to withhold America's track and field athletes from Berlin, although Brundage and Baillet-Latour had spoken of running an end-around through the AOC, if necessary. It never came to that. By the slender margin of 58.25 to 55.75, the full membership of the AAU voted against a resolution calling for a firsthand investigation of conditions in Germany, after which it adopted a resolution that approved American participation "with the weak caveat that this action should not be interpreted as support for the Nazis."[17]

Brundage's victory became complete when the former AAU president was reelected, displacing Mahoney. A couple of weeks later, according to Lucas, Garland sent a note of congratulation to Brundage: "I am glad that you got Mahoney's scalp."[18]

Boycott efforts elsewhere, while never reaching the level they did in the United States, fizzled after it became clear America was participating. Teams from forty-nine nations, an Olympic record, made preparations for Berlin. Although some prominent individuals from several countries staged personal protests, there was no mass exodus even among Jewish athletes.

Having gotten his way, Brundage turned his attention to fund-raising, which had been neglected during the boycott controversy. Remarkably, the man sought significant contributions from the Jewish-American business community. Large reported:

> In March 1936 he wrote a heavy-handed letter to the advertising magnate Albert Lasker, advising him that the best way for the Jews to atone for their sins and to combat anti-Semitism at home was to get on board financially for Berlin: "The great and growing resentment in athletic circles in this country against the Jews because of the activities of certain Jewish individuals and groups in seeking to prevent American participation in the Olympic Games next August, should be offset by some action on the part of prominent organizations or individuals of your race. . . . My suggestion now is that . . . some Jewish group or committee assists the American Olympic Committee in its campaign to finance the American team. If the record showed contributions from $50,000 to $75,000 from Jewish sources it might be useful in the future."
>
> Lasker, to his credit, refused to be blackmailed, responding: "As an American, I resent your letter and your subtle intimations of reprisals against Jews. You gratuitously insult not only Jews but millions of patriotic Christians in America, for whom you venture to speak without warrant, and whom you so tragically misrepresent in your letter."[19]

Understandably, Brundage was very well received at the IOC's 35th congress that opened on July 29 in the auditorium of Berlin's Friedrich Wilhelm University. There, acting on a motion by countryman William May Garland, the body expelled Ernest Jahncke, the only American member to have taken a stand against the Berlin Games, for what was said to be his poor attendance records. Whether in defiance or out of habit, Jahncke was a no-show at the session.

Putting the entire affair into perspective was the choice to fill Jahncke's seat. It was none other than Avery Brundage, who would remain at the IOC table for the next thirty-six years, including the final twenty as president.

# CHAPTER 13

# Last Voyage

The SS *Manhattan* was a major upgrade over the SS *President Roosevelt*. At 24,289 gross tons, the pride of the United States Lines was almost twice the size of the ship that ferried the American Olympic team to the Netherlands eight years earlier. Four years after its maiden voyage, it offered the fastest transatlantic service in its class, eight decks, beds for more than 1,100 passengers, and a crew of 478.

It also had a reputation for luxurious accommodations in first (cabin) class, which were assigned to American Olympic Committee officials, coaches, and chaperones as well as journalists and celebrities—such as playwright and screenwriter Charles MacArthur, husband of actress Helen Hayes. The athletes, all 334 of them (48 had previously departed or were scheduled to leave later), were counted as second class citizens.

"As usual, the athletes were in what we called steerage and the Olympic Committee was up in first class," recalled Jim LuValle, a 400-meter runner from UCLA. "We weren't allowed up in first class. Sometimes, you tried to sneak up to go to the movies in first class, but as soon as a steward saw you they chased you out. We resented it very much."[1]

The caste system would figure prominently in what became the major story of the trip. Still, the staterooms were comfortable. Whereas Betty Robinson was a wide-eyed youngster on the voyage to Amsterdam, now she was among the older and more worldly members of the women's track and field team. So Dee Boeckmann, her roommate in 1928, assigned Robinson to bunk with Helen Stephens, 18, and Kathlyn Kelly, 16, the only two teenagers to qualify for Berlin, in cabin 35 on deck six.

"A floating hotel," Stephens wrote in her diary. "Very nice indeed."[2]

In addition to Robinson, there were two other veterans of Amsterdam on the ship, Anne Vrana O'Brien, who had married and given birth to a daughter in the interim, and Olive Hasenfus, selected as an alternate sprinter for the second time. Of the others, Annette Rogers, hurdlers Simone Schaller and Tidye Pickett, and sprinter Louise Stokes all qualified for the 1932 team, but neither Pickett nor Stokes—the first two African American females to be issued U.S. Olympic uniforms—had competed in Los Angeles.

When the *Manhattan* cast off for Hamburg from Pier 60 on the morning of July 15, 1936, there were nine first timers among the women, including, of course, the prospective star in Stephens. They all thrilled to the sights and sounds of the ceremony which, the United Press reported, resulted "in a bedlam of bon-voyage cheers from more than 10,000 well-wishers and an ear-splitting din from the tied-down whistles of harbor craft. It was probably the grandest and noisiest farewell New York ever knew. Ashore and afloat, and even in the air where airplanes and blimps soared and dipped, exuberance was so manifest it almost knocked your hat off. It was a virtual tornado of massed joy because the team was off to the games—'full strength'—after weeks of apprehensive uncertainty over financial shortages."[3]

On the first full day at sea, the athletes received their uniforms. Shortly thereafter they also were addressed by Avery Brundage. The president of the American Olympic Committee lacked the commanding presence of his predecessor, Douglas MacArthur, but there was no doubt he had total authority over amateur athletics as it related to the Olympic Games. He told the team, his team, that this would be an extraordinary Olympics, one that would be long remembered. And he reminded them that they would be required to take the Olympic oath during the opening ceremony, reciting it for them word by word. He also issued orders against gambling—apparently half a dozen poker and blackjack games were reported in cabins on the previous night—and overeating, which he said induced seasickness. Smoking and drinking, he said, were best left to the discretion of the athletes themselves since the committee "can't go around wet nursing more than 300 persons for the eight-day voyage."[4] According to a United Press report, Brundage was particularly incensed by the distribution of "vitriolic, anti-Nazi pamphlets" to some of the competitors' cabins.[5]

One of those cabins housed Stephens, Robinson, and Kelly. The papers called for a boycott of the "Nazi Games" to protest restrictions on Germany's Jewish athletes and secure amnesty for political prisoners. Boeckmann asked her athletes to turn over the material and presented, in exchange, a copy of *Amateur Athlete*, which carried a story about the invitations to Gretel Bergmann and Helene Mayer offered by the German officials as well as IOC member Charles Sherrill's confirmation that the host country would not discriminate against Jews.

The athletes soon settled into a training mode with whatever was at their disposal. The available equipment was similar to what Robinson and a few others recalled from 1928. There was a running track, a boxing and wrestling ring, and gymnastics apparatus and plenty of mats for somersaults, cartwheels, and jumping and diving practice. And, yes, another makeshift pool for the swimmers. Iris Cummings, a national breaststroke champion at 15, later reflected on the state of the pool:

> Well, how do you train athletes on a ship? There was just
> one swimming pool which was about 20 feet by 20 feet
> and nine feet deep. And they pumped the saltwater into
> it and it sloshed around as the ship rolled. But that wasn't

terribly safe so they hung rope netting down into the pool; that's how people could climb up the side.

The water had to be three or four feet below the deck because it would slop out, and the water was five to six feet deep. It was very small. And then there were the nets hanging down the sides. Well, they would get the breast-strokers and we'd swim for a while, and then they'd take us out and put the others in. . . . They used long pieces of rubber which they'd tie around our waists and then we'd swim and the coaches would hold us back. Sometimes, they tied them to a post.

. . . It wasn't exactly training in any sense of the word. Well, in ten days, you deteriorate top-level production anyway, as far as muscles and development and lung capacity. And then for the ten days or two weeks before that you'd been running around New York City in the heat trying to raise money for the Olympics, or trying to figure out where you were going to get some clothes to go. The Olympic Committee handed out about six uniform items, as I recall.[6]

In the first days at sea, a few became sick, including two members of the eight-oared crew from the University of Washington. Among the women's track and field team, Kelly, Pickett, and Stokes fell ill. Those with settled stomachs were treated to as much food as they had ever seen in one sitting. Leading the way were the male track and field athletes who had endured 100-degree weather at their try-outs in New York, sapping their strength, and were in no mood to heed Brundage's warning.

"One thing l had to watch was eating," said Archie Williams, a 400-meter specialist from the University of California. "A bunch of young kids and all of us finely tuned and well trained. Well, you get on that big ship, and the first thing they do is start feeding you. They have before-breakfast sweet rolls, and then they had breakfast off the menu. Before this we'd been eating in the Automat. And then came lunch and tea break, then supper, and at ten o'clock at night you could come down and pig out, just to top things off. I imagine I picked up about eight or nine pounds."[7]

Watching others eat sometimes offered a form of entertainment. "Jack Torrance, the shot-putter, weighed about 300 pounds," LuValle recalled, "and he had the appetite of a small bird. He virtually ate nothing. Lou Zamperini [the 5,000-meter runner] weighed about 105 pounds and he'd eat two steaks and anything else he could get every night for dinner. In fact, I think I remember he used to sit next to Jack because he got all of Jack's food as well as his own."[8]

In addition, the ship offered the usual diversions prepared for cruise customers. There were movies and dances, amateur hour entertainment, mock weddings, and mock funerals. And, with the repeal of Prohibition in the United States, the consumption of alcoholic beverages was considerably greater among athletes than it had been on the *President Roosevelt* eight years earlier.

No one took greater advantage of its availability, it appeared, than Eleanor Holm Jarrett. A 14-year-old sprite in 1928 at Amsterdam, the swimmer had won the 100-meter backstroke in Los Angeles four years later, then married singer and orchestra leader Art Jarrett and began singing in nightclubs with her husband. "I was everything that Avery Brundage hated," she recalled. "I had a few dollars, and athletes were supposed to be poor. I worked in nightclubs and athletes shouldn't do that. I was married. All of this went against his whole concept of what an athlete should be."[9]

But Jarrett also was an outstanding swimmer. She had set the world record for her event in 1935 and was the favorite to defend her championship in Berlin. David Wallechinsky chronicled her adventures on the *Manhattan* in *The Complete Book of the Olympics:*

> Now on her way to her third Olympics, married and used
> to a flashy and independent lifestyle, Eleanor did not take
> too well to the third-class accommodations and strict reg-
> ulations that had been arranged by the American Olympic
> Committee. She felt more comfortable in the first-class

section, which happened to be where the American officials were staying, as well as the press. On Friday, July 17, Mr. [Herbert] Maybaum of the United States Lines, which owned the S.S. Manhattan, invited Eleanor to attend a party he was throwing that night in the A-deck bar and lounge. She was the only team member invited. Quick to accept, she stayed up until six A.M., matching drinks with the sports writers. She had to be helped back to her cabin.

The next day there was much joking and wisecracking among the non-Olympic first-class passengers about the 'training techniques' of the U.S. team. Embarrassed U.S. Olympic officials issued Holm a warning, but she was defiant and continued to drink in public off and on for the next few days. When advised by friends to moderate her behavior, she reminded them that she was "free, white and 22."

On July 23, while the ship made a prolonged stopover in Cherbourg, France, with the passengers confined to ship, Holm attended an afternoon and evening champagne party. At about 10:30 P.M., the official team chaperone, Ada Taylor Sackett, discovered Eleanor staggering along the deck, accompanied by a young man. After returning to her cabin, which she shared with two other swimmers, Holm stuck her head out the porthole and began shouting obscenities. Her roommates, Olive McKean and Mary Lou Petty, pulled her back inside and convinced her to go to sleep. At midnight Mrs. Sackett returned with the team doctor, J. Hubert Lawson, and the ship's doctor. Dr. Lawson found Holm "in a deep slumber which approached a state of coma." His diagnosis: "Acute alcoholism." The physical examination failed to awaken her. Members of the American Olympic Committee met to discuss the charges against Holm, which also included shooting craps. (She never denied the charges and later boasted that she had won "a couple hundred dollars" just before the final party.)[10]

Brundage did not inform her directly that she had been removed from the team. Instead, he had team manager Herbert Holm (no relation) do the dirty work at 6 A.M. Even worse was the decision of the women's track and field coach to use Eleanor Holm Jarrett as an example.

"To show what happened to girls who ignored the rules, Dee Boeckmann paraded her team into Eleanor's stateroom," wrote Stephens's biographer, Sharon Kinney Hanson. "Eleanor was 'laying in' that morning, less than shipshape, and recovering from a 'headache.' Helen [Stephens] was horrified that her coach humiliated Eleanor that way. She commiserated with Betty, who also was sympathetic with Eleanor. They grumbled to each other, asking why their coach and old tight lace [Sackett] were being so hard on her."[11]

Later in the day, Jarrett pleaded her case to Brundage, through what was reported to be a crack in the door to his stateroom. Some 220 athletes signed a hastily distributed petition seeking her reinstatement. But when the *Manhattan* completed its trip down the Elbe River and docked in Hamburg, the swimmer was on her own.

The AOC president left her with a return ticket to New York. But Jarrett was not without resources, including a strong relationship with the press.

"Brundage tried to send me home, but he couldn't because the Associated Press hired me, and I had press credentials," Jarrett said. "It was Alan Gould [sports editor] of the AP who arranged all this. I wrote a column and I had some mighty fine writers [ghostwriting] it for me—writers like Paul Gallico, Alan Gould and Tom Walsh. I had the best time doing my column, and it went on the AP wire all over the country."[12]

So Jarrett witnessed the entire Olympics from a front row seat and the Nazis invited her to all the VIP parties, where she delighted in bumping into Brundage and his AOC cronies. "He would be so miserable because I was at all these important functions," she said. "I would ignore him—like he wasn't even alive. I really think he hated the poor athletes. How dare I be there and take away his thunder? You see, they all wanted to talk to me."[13]

Compared to Jarrett's adventures, the rest of the Olympians had relatively tame stories of the voyage. Travel veteran Betty Robinson did have her steam iron confiscated because it violated fire safety regulations, but that was as exciting as it got for the vast majority of athletes. The real drama lay ahead, from the moment they embarked in Germany to a crowd of well-wishers and an oompah band. First stop was Hamburg's city hall, where they were served fine wine in antique glasses. Next stop was the station where they boarded two special trains for the three-hour ride to Berlin.

More bands awaited them in the cavernous confines of Lehrter Railway Station, and thousands of spectators jammed the streets leading to the city hall in Berlin, where the team was received by the mayor, leaders of the German Organizing Committee, the Reich sports commissar, and IOC president Baillet-Latour. Brundage was impressed, perhaps even touched, by the ceremony and the presentation of a commemorative medal.

"No nation since ancient Greece has captured the true Olympic spirit as has Germany," Brundage said. According to Arthur Daley, the correspondent for the *New York Times,* the statement raised a few eyebrows among American officials and athletes alike.[14]

Then it was on to the buses for the final leg of the journey. The men were dispatched to the new Olympic Village built and administered by the army amid a birch forest twenty miles outside the city. The women had the shorter ride to a dormitory, which the Germans called Friesenhaus, on the grounds of the Olympic Stadium and pool. As they stared out the windows, the curious athletes couldn't help but notice the rampant displays of swastikas on bloodred banners that decorated the main boulevards and the vast number of Germans, including youngsters, in uniform. The more observant sensed something unusual about the buses.

"I noticed they looked like military vehicles," said fencer Joanna de Tuscan, "and they had all sorts of places that looked like they might be for guns or whatever. And the wheels looked odd. That was the first thing I noticed. It was the first bus we were on when we arrived in Berlin. We were on this bus to be taken to the Olympic quarters. And I looked at this bus and I said to someone, 'You know, this looks like some sort of heavy duty military vehicle.' And every bus that we used looked like this."[15]

The weather was damp and chilly, a far cry from the sweltering New York they had left behind. The Spartan conditions of the Friesenhaus—each room contained two beds with straw mattresses, one dim ceiling bulb, and no hangers—combined with the gloom outside led the Americans to christen the building the "Freezin' House." The first breakfast of dark bread and green apples in the large dining hall brought hoots of protest from the American women, resulting in a change to bacon, eggs, cereal, and juice. They couldn't do much about the broadcasts from the floor radio in the lounge.

"At first the girls thought it would be 'swell' to be able to dance to big-band music. But the radio was receptive to one station only, airing Wagnerian operas, German marching songs and Hitler's daily volks sprechen—addresses to the people."[16]

What the facility lacked in style and comfort, however, it compensated in location. Stephens, Robinson, and their teammates could walk to the training track. The swimmers could stroll to the practice pool. And all the occupants could follow the pathway to the magnificent Olympic Stadium and gain entrance to any event with their competitors' badges.

After so many days of travel and so little exercise, the Americans needed workouts to regain their competitive edge. Although the cinder and red clay track was soft from the frequent bouts of rain, it was preferable to the *Manhattan*'s hard boards, which had contributed to Stephens's shin splints. Because of the latter, her limp matched that of Robinson when they started serious training in Berlin.

With the help of a German masseuse who treated her in the infirmary, Stephens's legs eventually regained their tone. She also practiced tossing the discus on a nearby field, although there was no one knowledgeable enough to help her with her untrained form. Stephens still found time for shopping in Berlin with Betty, Kathlyn Kelly, and Dee Boeckmann.

One week after landing on German soil, the complete American

Olympic team assembled on the May Field outside the massive stadium and under the celebrated airship *Hindenburg*, which flew the Olympic flag from its gondola as well as a swastika from each tail fin. They were waiting for Hitler and a moment in time they would never forget.

# Torch Song

After the Nazi high command decided that the public relations value of hosting the Olympic Games trumped the cost and inconvenience of welcoming foreign citizens into their midst, they sought new avenues in which to exploit the world competition. Foremost in the minds of Joseph Goebbels, the propaganda minister, and his staff was the Olympic torch relay.

By lighting the Olympic flame—introduced at Amsterdam in 1928—with the fire from the site of the ancient Games in Greece, the Nazis could boast of a connection with the spirit of the original competition while parading their ascendency through parts of Europe on which they had grand designs. They mapped out a plan that would cover some 3,000 kilometers in twelve days, requiring more than three thousand runners who, once inside the borders of Germany, were required to fit the Aryan ideal of blue-eyed and blond. According to David Clay Large,

> The 1936 Olympic torch relay was an "invented tradition"
> within the invented tradition of the modern Olympic
> Games. There had been no such torch relays in the ancient
> games or, for that matter, in any of the ten official modern

Summer Olympics preceding the Berlin games. The torch relay was but one of many ways in which the Nazi games helped define the modern Olympic experience as we know it today. In contrast to the essentially innocuous Olympic torch relay spectacles that have become familiar to us in recent years, however, the original German relay did more than simply promote interest in the upcoming games: It carried some very heavy ideological baggage.

Initially proposed by the Nazi Propaganda Ministry, and orchestrated primarily by Carl Diem, the indefatigable secretary-general of the German Organizing Committee, the relay turned into an advertisement for the new Germany across southeastern and central Europe, a region coveted by Nazi proponents of *Lebensraum* (living space)—and eventually overrun by the Wehrmacht. The seemingly innocuous torch trek from Olympia to Berlin prefigured the naked aggression to come. At the same time, as if to provide an illustrious pedigree for the new German empire envisaged by Hitler, the relay quite overtly and ostentatiously posited a symbolic bridge between modern Germany and classical Greece.[1]

The opening ceremony of the Games was set for four o'clock on the afternoon of August 1. In the morning, members of the International Olympic Committee gathered at the Lustgarten along with Adolf Hitler, Joseph Goebbels, the Reich air minister Hermann Göring, other chief deputies, and thousands of Hitler Youth to welcome the torch from Greece. Arriving on schedule, the runner jogged down the center aisle of the great square, lit a flame at the Old Museum, and ignited a second flame at the Royal Palace.

According to David Large, IOC president Baillet-Latour then thanked Hitler for the preparations made by Germany for the Games: "'All those who appreciate the symbolism of the sacred flame which has been borne from Olympia to Berlin are profoundly grateful to Your Excellency for not only having provided the means of binding the past and present, but also for having contributed to the progress of the Olympic ideals in future years.' In response Hitler thanked the IOC for the opportunity to host a festival whose purpose was the 'strengthening of human understanding.' As further proof of Germany's commitment to the traditions and ideals of Olympism, Hitler announced that the German government would resume and conclude the excavations at ancient Olympia that German scholars had undertaken between 1875 and 1881. He called this undertaking 'a permanent memorial to the Festival of the Eleventh Olympiad, Berlin, 1936.' "[2]

By the time of Hitler's arrival at the stadium, all the spectators had been seated and the 170 buses ferrying the male athletes from the Olympic Village had deposited their charges. "I remember we were all lined up outside the stadium," recalled Malcolm Metcalf, an American javelin thrower. "All the nations were lined up and then Hitler and his entourage of about 15 or 20 officials came out of a little gate and walked down the middle of that. All the Americans, of course, broke ranks and rushed up to get a good look. I got to look at Hitler from about 15 or 20 feet away. . . . He looked a little bit disturbed when he saw all these people rushing towards him. But he was well surrounded. He didn't need to worry."[3]

The Führer, in military uniform, entered the stadium from the Marathon Gate, flanked by Count Baillet-Latour and Theodor Lewald, both in formal wear. A fanfare from sixty trumpeters atop the stadium towers accompanied his appearance. "At his coming these assembled thousands rose to their feet, with their arms outstretched and voices raised in a frantic greeting," reported Frederick T. Birchall of the *New York Times*. "Massed bands blared a Wagner march."[4]

Spectators continued standing as Hitler and his entourage walked across the field to the Honor Lodge while the bands played "Deutschland Über Alles," the traditional German hymn, and the "Horst Wessel" song, the Nazi anthem. As the notables—which included Mr. and Mrs. Charles Lindbergh—took their places, there sounded a deep note from the Olympic bell with the inscription

"I summon the youth of the world." Immediately, the Greek team emerged from the archway below the stone staircase from which the Führer had descended. Then, noted Birchall, the *New York Times* European correspondent:

> They marched in a procession once around the arena, saluting the dais, each nation according to its custom, as they passed; then, turning across the field they took their stand in columns great and small in front of the Führer and the guests of honor, their flags at their head.
>
> Quite naturally, in this long march the interest was centered on the applause given respectively to each and the type of salute each nation gave the dais. The last item wasn't easily determined because the Olympic and Nazi salutes are very similar, the former being with the right arm stretched out sideways or nearly so from the shoulder, and the latter with the arm being stretched out in front.
>
> Nevertheless, the crowd carefully noted each salute as indicating the degree of sympathy for the Nazi regime. . . . In turn also the mode of saluting had a manifest influence upon the volume of applause received.
>
> In general the salutes stood about equally divided between the Olympic and Nazi, but "eyes right," with some individual modifications, was common to all. The Americans provided their own special salute by giving eyes right and placing their straw hats over their hearts.

The U.S. team, following its own tradition, was the only one which declined to dip its flag as it passed the dais. But before the crowd could react, the standard and flag of the host nation marched through the Marathon Gate and the band broke into "Deutschland Über Alles" and the "Horst Wessel" song. As a result, the *Times* noted, "The audience, rising promptly, froze in silent attention, so that the Americans marched, not to applause but to the tune of these two German national anthems."[5]

Decked out in white yachting caps and white suits, with an eagle emblem on their jacket pockets, the Germans goose-stepped eight abreast with military precision behind a swastika banner. Stretching their arms in the Nazi salute as they passed the Führer, they shouted, "Sieg Heil! Sieg Heil! Sieg Heil," then joined the other assembled athletes in the infield.

Although a man of a few thousand words, Hitler was limited in his role as head of state to a simple declaration. So Lewald, the head of the German Organizing Committee, took the occasion not only to welcome the athletes but to praise his chancellor "as the protector of these Olympic Games to be held in this stadium, built according to your will and purpose" and underline the dubious connection between Germany and the ancient Greeks.[6]

He spoke in German for almost twenty minutes, sounding, in the words of the *Times,* "the one lone discordant racial note" in the entire proceedings.

"In a few minutes," Lewald said, "the torch bearer will appear to light the Olympic fire on his tripod, when it will rise, flaming to heaven for the weeks of this festival. It creates a real and spiritual bond of fire between our German fatherland and the sacred places of Greece founded nearly 4,000 years ago by Nordic immigrants."[7]

Only then did he call Hitler to the microphone, where, adhering to Olympic protocol, he said in German, "I proclaim open the Olympic Games of Berlin, celebrating the eleventh Olympiad of the modern era."[8]

With that announcement, the ceremony proceeded to a second stage of audio and visual grandeur. Trumpets sounded another fanfare and a 21-gun salute rang out in the distance as sailors raised a giant Olympic flag to the top of the main flagpole, and flags of all the competing nations were similarly lifted into place atop the stadium. Seconds later, a delegation of Hitler Youth opened the doors to several hundred cages arrayed around the edges of the arena, releasing thousands of white pigeons—stand-ins for doves of peace. The pigeons swooped around the stadium and flew away while the Olympic Symphony Orchestra and a 1,000-member chorus dressed all in white began the "Olympic Hymn," composed specifically for these Games by Richard Strauss. Germany's foremost composer, at his own request, served as the guest conductor.

As the music faded, the last of the three thousand torch runners who had traveled from Greece through Bulgaria, Yugoslavia, Hungary, Austria, and Czechoslovakia appeared atop the steps of the East Gate. Later identified as Fritz Schilgen, 29, a former middle-distance runner, he had received the honor of providing the most anticipated moment of the opening ceremony. He paused briefly, then loped down the steps, across the field, and then up the stairs at the far end to a platform halfway to the top. He touched the torch to a black bowl set upon a tripod, and the Olympic flame flared. Seconds later, Schilgen bounded up the rest of the stairs and disappeared from view.

That was the signal for the flag bearers of the competing nations to gather in a semicircle around Rudolf Ismayr, a weight lifting champion from the 1932 Games. With one hand on the swastika-adorned flag of Germany, he swore the Olympic oath on behalf of all athletes: "We swear we will take part in the Olympic Games in loyal competition, respecting the regulations which govern them and desirous of participation in them in the true spirit of sportsmanship for the honor of our country and the glory of sport."

Before the recessional began the Nazis added an additional exercise to hammer home the point that Germany was the true heir to the Greek legacy. Spyridon Louis, the sheepherder whose inspiring victory in the marathon was the individual highlight of the first modern Olympics in Athens forty years earlier, was escorted to Hitler's box, where he presented the Führer with a sprig of wild olive from the sacred grove on Mount Olympus.

"I present to you this olive branch as a symbol of love and peace," said Louis, dressed in a traditional national costume. "We hope that the nations will ever meet solely in such peaceful competition."[9]

Displaying no sense of irony, Hitler thanked the aged runner and shook his hand, after which the choir commenced singing the "Hallelujah Chorus" from Handel's *Messiah* and the athletes filed out of the stadium in the reverse order of their entrance.

That should have been enough pomp and circumstance for any opening day but the Nazis weren't through. After nightfall, ten thousand performers took part in "Olympic Youth," a five-act pageant written by Diem. The athletes were back in their quarters preparing for the first day of competition, but thousands of spectators were treated to various dances and gymnastic routines performed to classical music. The stadium was lit by torches and searchlights, offering an otherworldly experience.

Apparently, even those anticipating shock and awe were overwhelmed. In their belief that nothing succeeds like excess, the Nazis may have been ahead of their time. Consider the impression they made on Birchall, the correspondent for the *Times*.

"The Olympic Games have had an opening notable even beyond expectations, high as these were," he wrote in conclusion. "They seem likely to accomplish what the rulers of Germany have frankly desired from them, that is, to give the world a new viewpoint from which to regard the Third Reich. It is promising that this viewpoint will be taken from an Olympic hill of peace."[10]

Goebbels himself could not have issued a more favorable summation.

# CHAPTER 15

# Power Play

Germany had been an indifferent participant in previous Olympic Games. Only in 1928, when it finished a distant second to the United States in overall medals, did it register among the top five nations. And it had never earned a gold medal in the signature events of men's track and field.

Clearly, that had to change if the Nazis were to project the image of an awakening power. It wasn't enough to demonstrate their great organizational skills to other countries. They had to beat them as well. According to David Large:

> In announcing his ambitious building program for the
> 1936 Berlin games, Hitler declared, "Buildings alone will
> not suffice to guarantee a showing by our athletes that is
> commensurate with Germany's world importance. More
> decisive here is the nation's unified commitment to pull-
> ing together the best [athletes] from all regions, and then
> schooling and hardening them, so that we [as a nation]
> can perform honorably in the upcoming competition."
>     By performing "honorably" Nazi Germany could show
> the world that its commitment to breeding and training

a new elite of athletic warriors was rendering the entire nation physically and spiritually superior to the "soft and decadent" Western democracies.[1]

While Hitler and his deputies were rebuilding the country's military might, they initiated a comprehensive program to identify and support the nation's best athletes in Olympic sports. That included female athletes even though the Nazis preached that a woman's place was in the home. Still, the lone gold medal achieved by a German track and field athlete belonged to Lina Radke, winner of the controversial 800-meter race in Amsterdam.

Hitler expected immediate improvement when he returned to the stadium for the first day of competition, and he was not disappointed. Tilly Fleischer, a Fräulein who had finished third behind Babe Didrikson in Los Angeles, claimed the first gold medal of the Games with a toss of 148 feet, 3 inches in the javelin. Later in the afternoon, Hans Wollke, a 25-year-old policeman, upset world-record holder Jack Torrance, from Baton Rouge, Louisiana, in the shot put. Of the first three events decided on day one, the Germans failed to win only the 10,000 meters, which resulted in an expected 1-2-3 sweep by the Finns.

So delighted was the Führer that he summoned all three winners to his box to offer his congratulations even though it delayed the program. But a fourth medal was awarded before the competition was over and Hitler did not stick around for the ceremony or send for the winner. Cornelius Johnson, a six-foot-five Californian who didn't remove his sweatsuit until the bar was raised to 6 feet, 6¾ inches, led an American sweep in the high jump that concluded at dusk with an Olympic record of 6 feet, 8 inches.

Johnson was the first of six African Americans on the U.S. men's track and field team to earn an individual gold medal, and Hitler's decision to ignore his victory after the public embrace of the other three was a conspicuous insult. It also represented more than a one-day story, because Jesse Owens, the acknowledged star of the U.S. squad, had easily qualified for Monday's semifinals in the 100 meters. He would be on center stage the following afternoon.

Baillet-Latour, the IOC president, reached out to intermediaries and asked them to inform Hitler that it violated Olympic protocol for the head of state to glad-hand the winners. Just in case the Führer did not take kindly to the suggestion, he said if Hitler chose to continue the practice, he must congratulate all of them without exception.

Hitler opted for none, which meant he didn't make a conscious decision to snub Owens on August 3 when the man coasted to victory in his semifinal heat and outraced Ralph Metcalfe, another member of what the German press derided as America's "black auxiliaries," for the gold medal. The Führer had to restrain himself when Karl Hein, a Hamburg carpenter, led a 1-2 German finish in the hammer throw.

On the same day, without the same level of attention paid to Owens and Hitler, Helen Stephens and Stella Walsh appeared on the same track for the first time since Stephens's stunning victory in the 50-meter dash at the 1935 national AAU indoor championships in St. Louis seventeen months earlier. The two hadn't set eyes on each other until the previous day when both sought treatment for their legs in the infirmary. No words were exchanged.

Stephens wasn't pressed in her 100-meter preliminary heat, which she won by at least 10 yards, or in her semifinal. The German fans were encouraged that three of their runners—Marie Dollinger, Käthe Krauss, and Emmy Albus—finished first in their initial heats. But none of them broke the 12-second mark, while Stephens ran world-record times of 11.4, wind-aided, and 11.5 seemingly without great effort. The other preliminary winners were Eileen Hiscock of Great Britain and Walsh, whose 12.5 was among the slowest of the winners. In fact, Dollinger edged Walsh in the second semifinal, although both were clocked in 12 flat.

Annette Rogers also qualified for the final with a third-place semifinal finish behind Dollinger and Walsh. The third American entry, Harriett Bland, washed out in the preliminary round.

To track fans, Walsh appeared to be saving something for the final, doing just enough to advance. But it was Stephens who had the heavier workload. In addition to the 100-meter final the next day, she was entered in the discus.

Although the weather on Tuesday was dismal, America enjoyed its greatest day on the track. Owens won the long jump with the help of a suggestion by German rival and runner-up Luz Long, Pennsylvanian John Woodruff held off Mario Lanzi of Italy to win the 800 meters, and Glenn Hardin of Louisiana continued his mastery of the 400-meter hurdles. And Stephens, while slipping and sliding to a tenth-place finish in the discus won by Fräulein Gisela Mauermayer, was in fine running form.

"I could see Stella digging in over there," Stephens told her biographer, Sharon Kinney Hanson, "digging her hole, getting ready to run against me. I really was beside myself with anxiety; I just didn't concentrate on the discus the way I should have." Relieved after making her last throw, she quickly made her way to the track and carved a place for her size-12 foot with a trowel.

"When the official's gun went off, Helen shot from the mark like a kid's bottle rocket, leaving behind nothing but the awed expressions of onlookers, the strained and smoky configurations of her would-be contenders," wrote Hanson. "She flashed light yards ahead of cocky Stella, left way behind Käthe Krauss, Marie Dollinger and her teammate, Annette [Rogers]. Emmy Albus was hardly an afterthought. She was far ahead of all of them.

"New Olympic and world titles were hers—the moment was hers, once her foot left the ground."[2]

In cold, blowing rain, she equaled her world record time of 11.5 set the previous day. Walsh was two meters behind in 11.7, Krauss third in 11.9. Rogers finished fifth, behind Dollinger and ahead of Albus.

Before receiving the gold medal in full view of the stands, Stephens extended her hand to Walsh and the two shook while the crowd cheered the sportsmanship. What followed may have been the most bizarre moment of the entire Olympics, orchestrated by none other than the short man with the mustache. Whereas Hitler wanted little to do with the mercurial Owens, he seemed fascinated by the tall American teenager who overwhelmed opponents of the other gender.

This did not come as a surprise to Stephens. According to Hanson, Stephens said, "Before I had gone over to Germany I had read quite a bit about him. I had read *Mein Kampf,* and I figured that somehow or another I was going to meet him. I just felt it was in the cards."[3]

So she was not surprised when one of Hitler's aides approached them as they walked off the field and asked her to follow him to the Führer's box. She said she would after she met with the press and sat for a radio interview broadcast back to the United States. The aide appeared apoplectic, but Stephens and Boeckmann breezed by while the flustered man waited for them. Hanson documented what followed in *The Life of Helen Stephens: The Fulton Flash:*

> Quickly, he ushered them to Hitler's private room—a small glass-enclosed room behind his seating box. There, the three waited. Within minutes, the heavy red drapes covering the doorway parted and a dozen Blackshirts entered. They circled the room, posting themselves at the entry and along the walls, and then began unholstering their pistols. As they stood at attention, Helen and Boeckmann glanced at each other and at the troopers, wondering what would happen next.
>
> Then two armed soldiers stepped in ahead of Hitler, who was followed by two more. In dress military uniform, with five-inch swastikas on each sleeve, black boots and brass buttons, Hitler crossed the crowded room, faced Helen and saluted. "It was sloppy," Helen said, "like he didn't really want to give me one." She extended her hand for a handshake. He grabbed it and pulled her toward him, patted, pinched and hugged her. "Of course, wearing that hat, he looked taller," Helen said, and he behaved in an uncomfortably familiar way. She thrust her autograph book into Hitler's hand, and his interpreter, deputy Rudolf Hess, explained that she wanted his autograph. Helen gave this account as Hitler signed her book:
>
> "A little guy wearing a uniform and a press identification tag snaps a picture. I never saw a man change his dis-

position so fast as Hitler did. And as the camera flashed, Hitler jumped about two feet in the air. When he landed, fists flaying, he bellowed something like, 'Was fällt Ihnen ein? Get him! Destroy the evidence!' Hitler's face turned red, and his eyes fumed hatred and rage.

"Dee screamed back, 'Don't you dare!'

"While guards restrained the photographer, Hitler slapped his leather gloves across the man's face, then punched him and kicked his shins, all the while screaming in German.

"Dee pulled back a few steps out of the way and whispered, 'I think he just set a new high jump record.' In the scuffle, the camera fell to the floor and Hitler booted it like a football against the wall. Then, guards hiked the guy— one, two, three—through the door. One guard picked up the smashed camera and tossed it after him. Another retrieved one of Hitler's gloves that lay near Dee's feet. Hitler calmly turned to me, smiled sweetly as though nothing had happened. He wriggled his body as if to shake himself back into composure. Hess said to me, 'I thought Miss Boeckmann didn't understand German.' When Hitler spoke again, his eyes fixed on mine, and his sentences came soft and controlled. Hess' voice quivered. 'Fräulein should consider running for Germany. Fair hair, blue eyes. Strong, big woman. The Chancellor says you are a pure Aryan. Yes?'

" 'Nein, Danke,' I shook my head and smiled back at Hitler. Still looking at me, Hitler asked through his interpreter what I thought of Germany and its progress. 'You like Berlin better than Fulton homeland?'

"I said, 'Yes, Mr. Hitler, Berlin's very, how do you say, nice, pretty? Schoen? Even in the rain.' I kept my comments short, positive. Hitler beamed. What I had seen in Hamburg and Berlin looked good—the Third Reich made sure Berlin had put her best foot forward for her international visitors. I didn't want to discuss the heck of a depression we were experiencing in the 1930s.

"'Fräulein Stephens, no one will ever break your record,' Hitler said [through Hess], but I told him that records are meant to be broken.

"'You would like to spend the next weekend with Chancellor Hitler at his villa in Berchtesgaden?' Hess asked.

"Dee spoke up again, 'Tell your Führer Miss Stephens is in training. The relay's next Monday. Thank him for her, but Miss Stephens can't.' When Hitler realized the answer, he turned to Dee. Again his face broadened into a smile as he waited for the interpreter. 'Would she join him in Berchtesgaden?'

"And Dee said, 'Thank you, Chancellor. Duty demands much, no?' addressing her refusal this time directly to Hitler. 'Thank you, but no, I too cannot accept your kind offer.' Hitler seemed to understand before his translator gave him her answer. Then he reached behind me, pinched, then saluted us both and marched out."[4]

That constituted the only private meeting between an American athlete and the Führer and she had the picture to prove it. Much to her surprise, the image of Stephens with Hitler appeared on postcards sold at booths around the stadium the following day. The teenager bought a half dozen and the photo was reprinted around the world.

But that wasn't the end of her association with Nazi officials. She was invited along with her coach and teammates Betty Robinson, Harriet Bland, and Kathlyn Kelly to a VIP celebration that night. They partied with Germany's social and political elite, Goebbels and Göring among them, as well as Charles MacArthur and his wife, Helen Hayes, Eleanor Holm Jarrett and her husband, Art, Avery Brundage, composer Richard Strauss, Olympic filmmaker Leni Riefenstahl, and boxer Max Schmeling.

The next afternoon, while Jesse Owens claimed his third individual gold medal in the 200 meters, Boeckmann began planning for the 4 × 100-meter relay that started on August 8 and would culminate the following day. Germany, which had placed three women in the 100-meter final and which had been practicing as a unit for an entire year, was considered the heavy favorite. The coach had a surprise in store for that team but first she had to select the four runners best qualified to fashion an upset. The men's 4 × 100 team also had questions to answer but they were entirely internal since the United States was a prohibitive favorite no matter which among its deep field of sprinters were chosen for the task.

The intrigue would continue throughout the week and set the stage for two remarkable performances that concluded the track and field portion of the Olympic Games.

# CHAPTER 16

# Third Reich, Third Medal

If there were any indecision about the identity of the anchor for the U.S. women's relay team—and there is nothing to suggest Dee Boeckmann hesitated for so much as a second—it was obliterated by Helen Stephens's performance in the 100-meter dash. True, she had no experience in the teamwork that such an endeavor required. But she was so much faster in running the distance than any of her competitors that the coach's competence, if not her sanity, would have been questioned if she looked elsewhere.

That didn't mean Boeckmann couldn't pretend otherwise, couldn't attempt to misdirect the opposition. When America's relay team reported to the practice track two days before the semifinal heat on August 8, the coach unveiled her plan to the four runners. First, of course, she had to name her selections, at least in one case an unpleasant task.

She wanted both Betty Robinson and Nettie Rogers. Not only had they both participated in Olympic relays but they had competed together at various meets in the previous two years. They also ran the fastest time trials, other than Stephens, during the days they had spent in Berlin. Of the five other possibilities for the last spot, two were particularly insistent on filling the opening.

Tidye Pickett, the 21-year-old from Chicago, already had become the first black woman to represent the United States in track and field when she began the 80-meter hurdles. But after advancing in the first round, she clipped a hurdle in her semifinal heat and fell on her shoulder, eliminating her from the competition. That was on August 5, the day after Stephens's victory in the 100 meters.

The injury served to make Harriet Bland bolder in making her case. Bland, also 21, had been eliminated in the first round of the 100-meter dash and had slower times than Pickett in time trials. But she was from St. Louis, Boeckmann's hometown, and had been trained by the coach ever since she was left off the 1932 team for, in her own mind, political reasons.

"Tidye's out because she's injured," Bland argued. "She had her chance. . . . I deserve this race. I'm not going to be cheated out of an Olympic medal again."[1]

"Harriet's not in peak condition, either," Pickett told Stephens, trying to play the role of conciliator. "Sick and coughing all over everybody. Coach is unfair and you know it."[2]

In the end, Boeckmann chose Bland. "Dee gave the race to her pet," Stephens conceded.[3]

The next order of business was the order of running. In practice, the coach decided to move everyone around. She had Stephens run the first leg, then run second after Harriett. She tried Betty in the anchor position with Stephens third.

"She [Boeckmann] told them that the German coach would be watching them," Hanson recounted in *The Life of Helen Stephens.* "Though the German team had favorable odds for winning, the Americans were expected to give the German girls tough competition. Dee wanted to psych the German coach into thinking she was uncertain about what lineup to use. She wouldn't tell a soul ahead of time what the final arrangement would be. Who best ran the first leg and who best ran the last could make the difference between which team would win and which would lose the race, that is, come in second. She knew it. The German coach knew it. And the girls, she said, had better know it, too! She told them that they all had better be ready to run their best regardless of what place they ultimately would run in."[4]

On the surface, the men's relay team had neither personnel problems nor the need to mask its intentions. Coach Lawson Robertson said that the services of Jesse Owens would not be required for the relay because, with gold medals in three events to his credit, he had "done just about enough in one Olympics."[5] According to an Associated Press dispatch, Marty Glickman, Sam Stoller, and Foy Draper were considered "certainties on the basis of trials the last few days" and that Frank Wykoff, a member of the gold medal relay team in both 1928 and 1932, would likely complete the team.[6]

According to *The Nazi Games,* "Glickman and Stoller, the lone Jews on the American Olympic track team, had been personally assured by Robertson that they would run, and they had spent the first days of the games assiduously preparing for the event. Recalled Glickman: 'For the ten days or so we were there before the race, we practiced passing the baton every day. Sam and I along with Foy Draper and Frank Wykoff. . . . Sam was the fastest starter, I had power down the straightaway, Foy could run the turn the best, and Frank was the seasoned veteran of the Olympic Games. That is the way we practiced and were coached.'"[7]

But at a team meeting on the morning of August 8, the day of the preliminary heats, Robertson told Glickman and Stoller that they were being replaced by Owens and Ralph Metcalfe, the first two finishers in the 100-meter dash. Robertson told the *Times* he had made the decision the previous night on the basis that the Dutch were a serious threat and that Germany had "quietly built up a quartet that had been clocked in a sensational time."[8]

Publicly, Owens was thankful for the opportunity. "That's swell news," he said. "I haven't known what to do with myself since Wednesday. I'll sure hustle around that corner."[9] In later interviews, Owens said he urged the coaches to run Glickman and Stoller instead of himself and Metcalfe. Metcalfe recalled Owens lobbying for a chance at a fourth gold medal.

"Whatever Owens did or did not say, Stoller and Glickman were devastated at the news of their removal," Large reported in *The Nazi Games.* "Glickman recalls insisting that Owens and Metcalfe were not needed because any foursome the Yanks put together could beat the Germans by 15 yards. . . . Glickman also recalls reminding the coaches that he and Stoller were 'the only two Jews on the track team,' and if they didn't run there was 'bound to be a lot of criticism back home.' "[10]

Stoller, from the University of Michigan, thought that the culprit was assistant track coach Dean Cromwell from the University of Southern California, who, once the decision had been made to employ Owens and Metcalfe, made sure his runners (Draper and Wykoff) were not replaced. Glickman, a Brooklyn native who ran for Syracuse University, was certain that Avery Brundage had pressured the American coaches to drop the pair so as not to further embarrass Hitler after so many victories by black athletes.

In his official report to the president at the conclusion of the Olympics, Brundage addressed that charge: "An erroneous report was circulated that two athletes had been dropped from the American relay team because of their religion. The report was absurd. The two athletes in question were taken only as substitutes."[11]

With virtually no time for practice, Robertson nominated Owens as the starter in place of Stoller and had Metcalfe run second, in Glickman's spot, leaving Draper and Wykoff in their accustomed positions for the first heat. Not surprisingly, the Americans breezed to victory. Their time of 40 seconds flat was more than a second faster than both of the other heat winners, the Netherlands and Germany, and equaled the Olympic and world records set by the 1932 U.S. team in Los Angeles.

A half hour later, the women's team made its first appearance in competition. Bland, Rogers, Robinson, and Stephens, in that order, ran a credible 47.1 in easily defeating Canada in the first heat. But what happened in the second heat caused everyone to reconsider America's chance in the final. The foursome of Emmy Albus, Käthe Krauss, Marie Dollinger, and Ilse Dorffeldt, which had set an unofficial record of 46.5 seconds before the Olympic Games, was timed in a sensational 46.4, a mark that would remain unbroken for 16 years, in the second heat.

For the men, the final was overkill. The U.S. team won as it pleased, setting a world record (39.8) that would last for 20 years while routing second place Italy (41.1). That quiet German quartet about which Robertson was so concerned finished a distant third, only because the Dutch fumbled the baton, which served to confirm everyone's worst suspicions.

According to the Associated Press report, "The 15-meter margin by which the Americans licked Italy . . . didn't appear to justify the eleventh hour lineup switch in which Ralph Metcalfe, Foy Draper and Frank Wykoff were named with Owens, and two Jewish boys, Sam Stoller of Michigan and Marty Glickman of New York, were dropped."[12] Stoller and Glickman were the only two healthy members of the men's track team not to compete in Berlin.

The women, however, provided a different story on a rare sunny afternoon. They played a leading role in one of the grand dramas of the Berlin Games. As she had on the practice track, Dee Boeckmann continued to move her runners around right up to the start of the final in an attempt to get the Germans thinking about their opponents rather than concentrating on their own assignments.

In her pre-race instructions, the coach told Stephens to line up for the third leg and Robinson to assume the anchor position. Once the German girls got set, the two Americans traded places as directed.

"Helen was now anchor," Hanson reported, "and the German coach and her girls appeared anguished by the last-minute change."[13]

As she had the previous day when her team set the record, the German coach placed her slowest runner last. Ilse Dorffeldt was 24, a Berlin native, and the only member of the quartet who had not qualified for the 100-meter dash.

The Germans, as expected, opened up a lead and then extended it as Albus passed to Krauss and Krauss gave way to Dollinger. By the time Dollinger passed the baton to Dorffeldt, the gap between the Germans and Americans was anywhere from eight yards to 10 meters depending on who was doing the counting. What happened next may have been the result of Dorffeldt's anxiety as she prepared to hold off the fastest woman in the world, or her fear as she waited to perform in front of 110,000 people, including the Führer, or her relative inexperience running anchor.

She had no problem grabbing the baton. It was what she did with it during her first few strides that sucked the noise out of the stadium.

"She received it all right," Stephens recalled, "but then dropped it when she exchanged it from one hand to the other. You didn't have to do that if you were running last, but she was used to running first. I saw that happening out of the corner of my eye, but I couldn't wait to appreciate it at the time."[14]

What would have happened had Dorffeldt hung on to the stick will never be known. In the official report filed with the IOC, the German organizers sided with their team. "The final race looked like a German victory because Albus had forged ahead of the field and Krauss and Dollinger had increased the lead to about nine meters at the time of the final exchange," it read. "It is doubtful whether even a Helen Stephens could have overcome such a handicap."[15]

Americans thought otherwise. "The chances were that the Reich would not have triumphed anyway," declared Arthur Daley in the *New York Times*. "Miss Dorffeldt could not have beaten Miss Stephens even with an eight-yard lift in the getaway. But it simplified matters for the Americans and left the Germans with the quaint delusion they would have had another gold medal had not the gods frowned at the wrong moment."[16]

Robinson had little doubt that Stephens would have overtaken Dorffeldt. "I wish the German girl had not dropped the baton," she said, "because Helen Stephens could run circles around those girls. . . . Helen would have won it for us even if the last German girl had not dropped the baton."[17]

Stephens certainly was sure of herself in the immediate aftermath of the race, which the United States won by a comfortable eight yards over Great Britain in the time of 46.9. "I felt that I could have chewed [Dorffeldt] up," she said in an interview five decades later. "But in retrospect, as the years pass, maybe I wasn't as fast as I thought I was. At the time, however, I thought it would have been a close finish."[18]

The spectators appeared as stunned as the German runners.

"The Reich's standard-bearers were at the head of the procession all the way and the spectators were going wild with joy when Marie Dollinger zoomed up to Ilse Dorffeldt eight yards ahead of Betty Robinson," Daley wrote. "To the Germans the championship already was won. They split the air with their cheers and then suddenly there was an awkward and embarrassing silence."[19]

In her authorized biography of Helen Stephens, Sharon Kinney Hanson detailed the aftermath. "In seconds, Helen flew past Ilse, opening about an eight-meter chasm between herself and the trailing British rival. Ilse, in a state of shock, was now crying, staggering off the track. Her teammates hovered around her; their eyes searched fleetingly for the lost baton and darted upward to the chancellor's box. Stunned like everyone else, Hitler had risen from his seat. His mouth gaped wide, his face winced in defeat. His arm stretched out, his finger pointing to where the baton had rolled to a stop."[20]

Although the Führer was furious with the outcome, he demonstrated compassion for the heartbroken German women. "Touched by the spectacle of Miss Dorffeldt crying bitter tears on the track there below," Daley wrote, "he had the four girls brought to his box where he consoled them with the remark that despite the fact they had not won any medals they had at least the satisfaction of knowing they were the best."[21]

Of course, the Americans had gained something more tangible. The victory enabled Helen Stephens to join Babe Didrikson as the only other woman to earn two gold medals in track and field at the same Olympics. It resulted in a second relay gold medal for Annette Rogers, who had run the third leg on the winning team in Los Angeles. And it completed a remarkable comeback for Betty Robinson, who, five years after a life-threatening plane crash, added a second gold medal to the one she had won as a carefree 16-year-old.

"She was a marvelous runner," Rogers recalled years later. "She still had the limp. But even on that relay team that girl ran with such fight, she was going to do her best."[22] The four Americans were ushered to the top step on the podium after the race. They all were crowned with laurel wreaths, presented with their gold medals, and treated to a rendition of "The Star-Spangled Banner" as the American flag was raised up the center flagpole. They all had reasons to be pleased and grateful.

But only one had the gratification of overcoming so much adversity. To Babe Robinson, who was so young and so unseasoned eight years earlier, it was almost as if her first Olympic triumph was something that happened to her. This moment was something she set in motion, she vowed to accomplish, she willed to happen, she savored.

"I had overcome so much to make the team, and I appreciated the fact that I did make it," she said in an interview five decades later. "I had to work very hard to make that team and the first just sort of fell into my lap. I was lucky the first time."[23]

"In 1928 I didn't have to work—just run. Nineteen thirty-six was different."[24]

Indeed, it was, on so many levels. Not only would there never be an Olympics quite like it, there would be no Olympics at all for the next dozen years thanks to later actions of the host nation. The Nazi Games would be the last until 1948.

# CHAPTER 17

## (Nazi) Party Time

For many of the athletes, the 1936 Olympic Games did not end with the closing ceremony. They culminated one night earlier with a party thrown by Joseph Goebbels, the minister of propaganda, at Pfaueninsel.

Throughout the Olympics, Hitler's competitive ministers had attempted to outdo each other by hosting extravaganzas for the elite among German citizens and foreign visitors. Because he held three titles—air minister, minister-president of Prussia, and president of the Reichstag—Hermann Göring had the privilege of staging three parties. The last and most lavish was an alfresco buffet for several hundred guests in a huge park surrounding Göring's house, followed by a Bavarian carnival that featured carousels, sideshows, and other amusements.

"In response, Goebbels took over the *Pfaueninsel,* Peacock Island, just below his new house on the Havel [River], for the final fling of the fortnight," wrote Anthony Read in *The Devil's Disciples: Hitler's Inner Circle.* "Army engineers provided a pontoon bridge to link the wooded island with the shore. He called on all the resources of the film industry to decorate it from end to end and to transform it into an enormous movie set, filled with pretty girls dressed as Renaissance pages—tabards and tights."[1]

Since all but a handful of events had been completed, Olympic teams were welcomed to the feast, which featured the Berlin Philharmonic, the Berlin Opera, and an enormous fireworks display. The effects were stunning.

"There were grassy lawns with the big tables with the white tablecloths with these collections of Rhine champagne sitting in the middle of the tables," recalled swimmer Iris Cummings, a wide-eyed 15 at the time. "There were bands and good food, marvelous service and a nice dinner. A few of the athletes consumed quite a bit of the champagne."[2]

Among the attendees were members of the victorious U.S. women's sprint relay team, most prominently double gold-medal winner Helen Stephens.

"They had about seven outdoor dance pavilions and bars with champagne running freely," Stephens said. "There were soldiers all over, standing at attention. During the course of the evening, a messenger came up to me and said, 'Hermann Göring wants to see you upstairs.' Harriet Bland and I said, 'Hey, this'd be a fun experience to go up there. We won't tell anybody.' Well we went up and there was a soldier in uniform standing before the door. Now this party was later written up by the press as one of those orgies, and that's what it was. We get inside the door and there's Göring sitting on a great big divan and a couple of gals sitting there in dubious attire. He had a table in front of them and I knew things weren't according to Hoyle when one of those girls slithered up from under the table. Then I realized that this black thing he had on was his kimono, and he was sitting there in his shorts."[3]

After Göring invited the Olympians to get more comfortable, he had to take a phone call, which gave the 18-year-old Stephens and her 21-year-old teammate an opportunity to depart the premises. "As I got ready to go out the door," Stephens said, "ol' Hermann Göring was still on the phone, and he jumps up and says, 'Auf Wiedersehen, Fräulein Stephens.' And he blew me a kiss—and that's the last I ever saw of him."[4]

Surely, it was a sendoff more memorable than anything offered at the stadium ceremony the following night, which Stephens spent attempting to cram souvenirs into her luggage while Robinson nursed a bad cold. Clearly, there was unintentional irony in the direction to which the Olympic Games were headed. After thanking German organizers for their "magnificent work," IOC president Baillet-Latour called on the youth of the world to assemble peacefully in four years in the next Olympic city—Tokyo.

Although they had been treated well by their hosts and the citizens they had encountered throughout Berlin, members of the American women's track and field team were eager to depart the following morning. "I was told to ignore the politics," Robinson recalled in a newspaper interview 45 years later. "We were there to compete and act like good American citizens. The Germans were very friendly and put on a beautiful show. But even then you could see the swastikas on the Jewish stores."[5]

Scheduled to compete in the International Women's Sports Festival, the ladies were whisked by bus to the train station for the trip to Wuppertal and a comfortable hotel where Helen and Betty drew the largest room.

They spent three nights in the hilly, medium-sized municipality in northwest Germany. After a city hall reception by local officials on the second day, they toured the zoo, the municipal gardens, and the suspension railroad, forerunner of the monorail, for which the city was celebrated. They also spent all their marks on whatever memorabilia they could find.

The meet drew 35,000 people, many focusing on a rematch between the U.S. and German 4 × 100-meter relay teams. Robinson, still battling a cold, was replaced by reserve Olive Hasenfus and the outcome was reversed but not because of the substitution. This time Dorffeldt hung on to the baton and the result was a dramatic finish in which both teams surpassed the winning mark at the Olympics.

In better weather and better track conditions than existed in Berlin, the Germans were clocked in 46.06 to 46.07 for the United States, with Stephens trailing Dorffeldt at the wire by a half meter. Otherwise, Stephens enjoyed a stellar night, defeating Stella Walsh at both 100 and 200 meters and taking second place in the shot put, a non-Olympic event.

They were up early the next morning to catch a 3:30 bus to Cologne, where, after eating breakfast at the airport, they flew to Paris. From there they boarded a train to Le Havre, where a ship was waiting to take them home to America. Although the SS *President Roosevelt* represented a step down in speed and comfort from the SS *Manhattan,* it was a sight for sore eyes to Robinson and Dee Boećkmann.

The pair would end their last Olympic venture on the boat that carried them to their first one in Amsterdam eight years earlier. Fittingly, Betty and Dee, joined by Helen, would occupy the same cabin in which they set sail for Europe in 1928.

Although the voyage was slow and rough, thanks to a combination of strong winds and fog, the trip was mostly enjoyable. There was no curfew, and wine and champagne flowed freely just as if Eleanor Holm Jarrett was in their company (she was not). Not only did the ladies sleep late, they occasionally enjoyed breakfast in bed.

On their third day at sea, the team treated Robinson to a formal dinner party in honor of her 25th birthday. The following night they attended a costume ball. And they all contributed their comic talents to a skit, which they staged for the other Olympians (a total of 199 returned on the *President Roosevelt*) lampooning their quarters in Berlin. Naturally, they called it "Freezin' House." Stephens was crowned by teammates for her performance and handed a bouquet of celery in place of flowers.

While several who did not medal felt left out and Tidye Pickett remained upset about the choice of Harriet Bland for the relay, the women's track and field team was a cheerful group compared to some of their fellow Olympians. No sooner had the ship docked than miler Gene Venzke sounded off against American officials whom he accused of being "petty, aloof and unfair" to the athletes. "They didn't mingle with us and spent a good deal of time squabbling among themselves," he charged.[6]

Three-time Olympian Dorothy Poynton Hill expressed similar

displeasure despite earning her second gold medal in platform diving. According to the *New York Times,* she groused, "I think that there wasn't a happy athlete on this Olympic trip."[7]

Certainly, New York did its best to cheer and cheer up the Olympians. Since the official welcome was scheduled to coincide with the return of the SS *Manhattan* from Hamburg—many members of the men's track and field team as well as other Olympians still were competing in Europe—the New York Hotel Men's Association offered free room and board for those who chose to wait around six days. Restaurateurs, theaters, and nightclub owners also welcomed the athletes who had already arrived. Not only was former heavyweight champion Jack Dempsey among those who greeted the ship, he issued an open invitation to his Broadway restaurant.

While the athletes made themselves available for press and radio interviews, they visited hospitals, attended baseball games—alas, Babe Ruth had retired the previous season—and toured the Empire State Building, including the 103rd floor observation deck, in the company of former governor Al Smith. Those who lasted the week joined the eighty-one Olympians arriving on the *Manhattan* at the 19th Street pier on the morning of September 3 for the full New York experience.

While the era of ballyhoo had passed, another victim of the Depression, and Grover Whalen had moved on to the presidency of the upcoming world's fair, the city still mustered enough excitement to stage its first ticker-tape celebration in three years. One hundred convertibles were lined up at Battery Park and Jesse Owens sat on the rear deck of the first car while Helen Stephens and Betty Robinson, along with several other female track athletes and their coach, shared the second automobile.

While the parade started at noon through the financial district, where the shower of paper was heaviest, it did not end at the traditional destination of city hall. It progressed all the way to Central Park, swung west and then north through Harlem, apparently in tribute to Owens and the other black stars of the track team, to the Triborough Bridge. The convoy stopped beneath the bridge at

Randall's Island, site of the men's track and field Olympic trials. After lunch, the athletes marched into the municipal stadium in their Olympic dress uniforms in the order, more or less, they had assumed in Berlin one month earlier.

They were met by Mayor Fiorello La Guardia, who hailed the Olympians as "splendid examples of American youth and American sportsmanship."[8] Alongside Dempsey and such other New York icons as dancer Bill (Bojangles) Robinson, marathon swimmer Gertrude Ederle, and former Olympians Mel Sheppard and Matt McGrath, the colorful mayor presented the athletes with medals struck for the occasion.

The award ceremony was broadcast nationally with such precision that the mayor's office was able to advise Chicago officials a day in advance of the time of Betty Robinson's participation.

"New York extends its hand in congratulations for the splendid part which your fellow townswoman Miss Elizabeth Robinson played in the 1936 Olympic Games," read the telegram from La Guardia's office to that of Chicago mayor Edward J. Kelly. "We are paying a well deserved tribute to her on Thursday, September 3, by presenting her with a commemorative medal of the City of New York. This program will be broadcast in your city from 3:30 to 4 P.M., Eastern daylight savings time. It occurs to me that you might wish to notify her friends and relatives so that they might share the joy of this occasion."[9]

For his part, Kelly dispatched a telegram to the Robinson household in Riverdale:

> Through the courtesy of the Honorable F. H. La Guardia,
> Mayor of the City of New York, I have been informed
> that your daughter will receive a commemorative medal
> tomorrow afternoon. I know you will be interested in
> listening to the radio broadcast of these ceremonies. I am,
> therefore, sending you a copy of the telegram received
> from Mayor La Guardia concerning the presentation.

>At this time, I want to express my appreciation of the
>honor that your daughter has brought to Chicago through
>participation in the Olympic games.[10]

In the only unscripted part of the ceremony, Owens gave away the first of his three individual gold medals, from the 100-meter dash. "An Olympic medal is the highest honor an athlete can win and I treasure mine above all my other possessions," Owens told the assembled crowd, "but I want to make a presentation to Bill Robinson, the [unofficial] mayor of Harlem, for all he has done for me, for all of us. I want to give him the first medal I won in the Olympic Games."[11]

There wasn't much time for Betty Robinson, Helen Stephens, or the other members of the women's relay team, Annette Rogers and Harriet Bland, to savor the festivities. Before the night was over, they were on a train for Toronto, where they were scheduled to run in two meets while Stephens had the additional task of racing at two distances against Canadian challengers.

The Canadian runners no longer were the world-class opponents they had been eight years earlier, and the relay team won as it pleased at Exhibition Stadium. So did Stephens at both 100 and 220 yards. They all enjoyed rides at the annual fair afterward. Two days later Stephens repeated her double victories, but the relay team wasn't so fortunate. This time the Americans gave the Canadians a gift similar to what the Germans provided in Berlin. The baton slipped from Rogers's hand as she prepared to hahd off to Robinson and the Yanks were disqualified. Fortunately, the only damage was to their pride.

From there it was back to New York and a final farewell to Olympic duty. Stephens had one more stop, a race in Washington, D.C., before driving back to Missouri with Boeckmann and Bland. Robinson and Rogers climbed aboard the train for Chicago and a quieter life.

There were no bands nor hordes of well-wishers at Union Station this time. Robinson was honored at the Elks club in Harvey, where Fred Steers of the American Olympic Committee paid her a tribute. One month later, on October 18, both Betty and Annette were recognized at a luncheon of the Illinois Club of Catholic Women, which had taken over the quarters of the Illinois Women's Athletic Club on North Michigan Avenue and which they had represented in track meets for the past year.

Among those attending the latter function were Edward J. Kelly, the mayor, and Avery Brundage, the Chicago industrialist who not only reigned as president of the American Olympic Committee and the AAU but now was an official member of the IOC. Far from being defensive about his role in the Nazification of the Olympic Games, he appeared heartened by the experience.

Just two weeks earlier, as recounted by Davis Maraniss, Brundage had participated enthusiastically in a German Day celebration at New York's Madison Square Garden:

> The event, run by a committee dominated by members of the American German Bund, an organization of German American citizens sympathetic to Nazi Germany, drew more than twenty thousand people. The honored guests included Karl Strolin, mayor of Stuttgart, who spoke of "the miracle which we owe to our leader Adolf Hitler and his unshakable belief in Germany." The German ambassador to the U.S., Hans Luther, said, "Germany is rearming not to make war but to make peace secure." When Brundage took the microphone, he defended the Olympics and praised Germany. No country since ancient Greece, he said, "has displayed a more truly national interest in the Olympic spirit in general than you find in Germany today." He thanked German Americans for helping fund the U.S. Olympic team when others threatened a boycott. "The question then was whether a vociferous minority highly organized and highly financed could impose its will on one hundred twenty million people." And he brought the huge crowd to its feet with a lesson he brought home from Berlin: "We can learn much from Germany. We, too, if we wish to preserve our institutions, must stamp out Com-

munism. We, too, must take steps to arrest the decline of patriotism."[12]

It was clear how Brundage felt about Nazi Germany. Soon thereafter, Nazi Germany demonstrated how it felt about Brundage. In 1938, his construction company received the contract to build a new German embassy in Washington, D.C. Alas, World War II intervened before construction could begin.

# Love and Marriages

From all appearances, Richard Schwartz and Betty Robinson had little in common. He was born in Cleveland to Jewish parents who had emigrated from Hungary. He attended prestigious Amherst College in the company of a fellow Clevelander, Burgess Meredith. He was not a varsity athlete.

But, like his future wife, Dick Schwartz was quick on his feet, so much so that he supplemented his country-club upbringing by teaching ice skating at the Elysium, which was the largest indoor rink in the world when it was built in 1907 and which provided live music at evening and weekend sessions. He also was a superb dancer, a talent which enabled him, in Betty's words, "to sweep me off my feet."[1]

He became acquainted with her story in 1929 when his family moved to Chicago and he saw her from afar when, seated in a wheelchair, she was introduced at a Northwestern football game. Not until the spring of 1939, however, did they meet at the urging of a mutual friend. It was the start of a relationship that would endure more than a half-century.

They attended movies, cocktail parties, and yes, dances. He introduced her to skating, an endeavor that was not entirely successful.

"It was fun being athletic together," she wrote. "But I better stick to running."[2]

Actually, in the years since her final Olympic appearance, she had considered a future in anything but. There was the prospect of modeling, for which she compiled a portfolio of glamour shots in the fashions of the day. She earned a reputation for her motivational speeches on behalf of women's participation in athletics and the Olympics. And there was a romance that led to an impulsive visit to city hall and a brief marriage to Eddie Napolilli, an elevator operator at a prominent Chicago hotel.

The union, kept secret not only from the public but from Betty's parents, was limited to weekend encounters. Although he said he couldn't live without her, he also didn't have the means to provide for her. After confiding in her family, she terminated the arrangement and filed for divorce.

Schwartz, who was a furniture buyer for the Spiegel catalogue, was not deterred by the circumstances. The waiting period for the state to act on her petition was in its second year and Robinson's case was expected to be heard before the end of 1939. Her 29-year-old suitor proposed in August, and they celebrated in September with family and friends at an engagement party in the renowned Pump Room of the Ambassador East Hotel.

One month later, Betty accompanied Dick to Cleveland, where she met many members of his family, including his older brother and sister and their spouses. "They all loved her," he told friends.

An elaborate ceremony was not an option for the couple because of the uncertainty and timing of the divorce. It wasn't until November 21 that she was called before Judge Rudolph Desort and asked to explain her charge of desertion. She said she asked her husband on several occasions to establish a home but he always replied, "I would if I could, but I can't."[3] The judge granted the decree, leaving Betty free to marry Dick.

They didn't wait long. Exactly ten days later, on the afternoon of December 1, 1939, they became Mr. and Mrs. Richard Schwartz in a private service at the parsonage of the First Methodist Church of Dolton, a few blocks from her Riverdale home. The maid of honor was Betty Mills, the 15-year-old daughter of her sister Evelyn, while Sandy Schwartz, Dick's brother, was the best man.

Ironically, if not symbolically, the 1940 Olympics, whose prospects were undermined by war in both Europe and the Pacific, were officially canceled by Count Baillet-Latour, president of the International Olympic Committee, the following day.

The former two-time Olympic champion had a new goal and a new partner with whom to chart the future. They moved into an apartment in Hyde Park, near the University of Chicago, and set out to start a family.

So much for all those Victorian fears espoused by some physical educators and physicians about athletics interfering with a woman's ability to bear children. The couple welcomed a son in 1942, and a daughter four years later. As the children—Richard and Jane—grew older, the couple purchased a house in the northern suburb of Glencoe, which boasted quality schools.

The Schwartzes agreed to disagree on certain matters. Betty continued to attend the annual Robinson gatherings at Stone Lake each summer, unaccompanied by her husband. She wanted to give her own children the same freedom from structure she had enjoyed in her youth—swimming, fishing, and unsupervised playtime with cousins. Dick, whose family was scattered geographically and less inclined to assemblies, preferred more upscale vacations. He also skipped the Christmas sing-alongs in Riverdale. Betty did drive Rick and Jane across the country to Beverly Hills, where Dick's mother and sister had settled after his father's death, one summer when Dick was delayed by work; he flew out to join them.

Dick had become a partner in a textile company that manufactured fabrics for furniture makers. But Betty wasn't content with raising money for future Olympics, serving as chairman of the Central AAU women's athletic committee, and officiating at occasional track meets. Not only was she approachable to the public, she preferred doing the approaching. Her children grew accustomed to her stopping total strangers on the street to compliment them on their appearance.

She took a position behind the counter at Knachman's candy shop in Hubbard Woods, close to the house on Linden Avenue. When the family moved to a larger house on Dundee Road on the north side of town, Betty changed her employer to a store that anchored the commercial center of Glencoe.

Wienecke's had been the biggest retail emporium in the area since the turn of the century, offering hardware, housewares, and even toys from a site on Vernon Avenue. Remarkably, it was the hardware that intrigued Betty Robinson. Even as a kid, she explained, she had wanted to work at a hardware store and she knew her screws from her nuts and bolts.

That's where she spent her days in a job as unpretentious as any sought by a former gold medalist. What's more, her home had few reminders of the Olympics. Beyond the framed "diplomas" awarded the medalists in Amsterdam and Berlin, the only suggestion of Betty's international triumphs was the pair of wooden shoes, adorned with autographs from 1928, at the side of the fireplace. A starter's pistol occupied a space in the hutch but that was associated with her volunteer work as a track official, not her personal athletic history.

The two gold and silver medals she earned at the Olympics were consigned to a Russell Stover candy box stashed in the hall closet, available for quick retrieval whenever she headed out the door to speak before students or other assemblies on the value of women's sports. Even in the 1960s, the avenues open to young women in athletics weren't much greater than they had been four decades earlier.

"The problem," she said, "is what to do with the girl who wants to compete. Opportunities for her are few, and she deserves the same chance that a mad dash for a train accidentally gave me."[4]

For most of her time in Glencoe, she was Mrs. Schwartz, the PTA mom, first and foremost. She volunteered for local charities, she swam, she golfed, and she bowled for recreation, just like many of her neighbors. Neither one of her children exhibited a driving ambition in track or other sports.

Still, there were occasional moments that set her apart. One occurred during a family vacation in New York when she was picked from a studio audience as a contestant in a short-lived game show, *Haggis Baggis*. In her brief television debut, she was awarded a stove by emcee Dennis James.

While she remained a popular figure in Chicago, national recognition continued to fade until November 1966, when she was honored by the Helms Athletic Foundation. Thirty-eight years after becoming the initial American woman to win an Olympic gold medal in track and field, she was enshrined in the Helms Hall of Fame, a California institution among the first of its kind in the country. The consensus of the Chicago papers: About time.

She also had to wait and wait and wait once USA Track and Field initiated its own Hall of Fame in 1974. The first class of twenty-six athletes, coaches, and officials featured two women, Babe Didrikson and the great Wilma Rudolph. Rudolph earned three gold medals at the Rome Olympics in 1960. The second class included a trio of females—Helen Stephens, Alice Coachman (the first African American gold medalist—high jump, 1948), and Stella Walsh, who received her naturalization papers in 1947 and won her last AAU title (senior pentathlon) in 1954 at the age of 43. In 1976, once more, Robinson was passed over while Dee Boeckmann, her teammate in 1928 and coach in 1936, was honored along with Mae Faggs, a three-time Olympian who won a relay gold medal in 1952 at Helsinki.

Finally, in 1977, the first U.S. distaff gold medalist was elected to the Hall of Fame in a class with Bob Beamon, Jackson Scholz, and Frank Wykoff.

By then, Betty and her husband were on the move to Naples, in south Florida. No sooner did they return to Illinois a few years later than Dick presented his wife with an award of his own. Once the state authorized the sale of vanity plates for motor vehicles, he secured the right to "Artemis," the mythic goddess to whom General MacArthur had compared Robinson in 1928. It was an identification she carried close to her muffler from that moment on.

A more disturbing reminder of the past occurred late in 1980 when Stella Walsh was killed by a stray bullet in Cleveland, bringing an abrupt and ironic end to the rivalry between the Polish-born athlete and Stephens. As David Wallechinsky recounted:

> After Stephens' victory in Berlin, a Polish journalist accused her of being a man, and German officials were forced to issue a statement that they had given her a sex check and that she had passed. Forty-four years later, on December 4, 1980, Stella Walsh went to a discount store in Cleveland to buy streamers for a reception for the Polish national basketball team. In the parking lot, she got caught in the middle of a robbery attempt and was shot to death. When an autopsy was performed afterward, it turned out that although Helen Stephens may not have had male sex organs, Stella Walsh did. All the while that Walsh had been setting 11 world records, winning 41 AAU titles and two Olympic medals, she was, in fact, a man.[5]

Technically, Walsh had ambiguous genitalia. Her cells contained both male and female chromosomes. Had officials known at the time, she would have been disqualified from the Olympics. But she lived her life as a woman. Robinson defeated her in their last race in 1931 and Stephens won all five races against Walsh before, during, and after the 1936 Olympics.

"I had no idea," Betty said, "but I always thought she was real masculine for a woman."

In any case, neither Robinson nor Stephens supported a movement to strip Walsh of her medals because of a birth defect. And while the IOC and other organizations considered the possibility of negating her records and titles, they eventually left intact her awards and achievements. Those included her place in the USA Track and Field Hall of Fame, whose officials chose only to add this caveat to her biography: "An autopsy revealed that Walsh had male sex organs."[6]

Robinson received an additional honor from Northwestern University, which listed her as a charter member of its sports Hall of

Fame. Although she never competed on the track for the school, she received extensive training from coach Frank Hill and considered the time she spent on campus as some of the most beneficial of her life. She was one of 11 among the chosen 25 able to attend the induction banquet in Evanston on February 4, 1984, and to be presented at halftime of a Northwestern vs. Illinois basketball game later that night. Seated alongside her was none other than Otto Graham, the greatest quarterback in Northwestern's history.

Annette Rogers Kelly, the woman who handed the baton to Betty at Berlin in 1936, was enshrined in 1985. Ironically, the Big Ten institution eliminated both the men's and women's track and field programs in 1988 for financial reasons, and the track at Northwestern's Dyche Stadium, the site of several Olympic trials, was removed during renovations in the following decade.

Robinson and Rogers, who achieved her friend's original goal of becoming a physical education teacher upon her graduation from Northwestern, were among the 15 track and field athletes from the 1936 Olympic team who assembled in Columbus, Ohio, in May 1986 for a fiftieth anniversary celebration. They were joined by their relay teammates, Helen Stephens and Harriett Bland Green, who had reunited for the first time at an Olympic Gold Medal Winners Celebration in Atlantic City in late 1979. This would mark the last time they would be together.

The reunion was held in conjunction with the fourth Jesse Owens Track and Field Classic at the man's alma mater, Ohio State University. All the women had an abiding respect for Owens. Stephens had run five exhibition races against him during the 1940s after both had been declared professionals. Once Owens moved to Chicago, where he started a public relations firm, he and Betty grew close and he was a frequent guest of the Schwartzes in Glencoe. "Really a nice man," she said.[7]

Owens certainly was on the mind of Dave Albritton, a silver medalist in the high jump at Berlin and a friend of the great sprinter since childhood. So was Adolf Hitler and his presence at the Games a half-century earlier. "As Jess used to say," recalled Albritton, who spent 16 years as a member of the Ohio House of Representatives, "'We went there to run and run we did, I'm here and I don't know where in the hell Hitler is.'"[8]

Unfortunately, Owens wasn't there in Columbus. He died from lung cancer in 1980. But the spirit that carried him to triumph in Germany infused the meet and the reunion.

# Home Stretch

By the time she acknowledged her 80th birthday, Betty Robinson had called a lot of places home. She had spent most of her married life in various suburbs on the north side of Chicago, had lived in two different areas of Florida, and had followed her daughter's family to Connecticut and then Colorado. But it was a grand occasion that drew her back to her roots.

When Riverdale celebrated its centennial in 1992, there was no more popular choice for guest of honor than the athlete who had brought it worldwide attention sixty-four years earlier. Although her father, mother, and two sisters all had passed on and different families occupied the three-flat at 3 East 138th Street, Robinson eagerly accepted the invitation to what the Riverdale centennial committee identified as a homecoming for its most famous citizen.

She never forgot where she came from or who had helped her become an Olympic champion. Just two years earlier she had attended the 100th birthday party for Charles Price, the teacher who told Betty she belonged on the track and opened the world to her, at his retirement home in Florida. Now she was returning to the company of old friends whom she hadn't seen in decades.

They included Florence Hedtke, her former teacher and later the principal at Bowen Elementary School a short walk from her home. The school had been demolished in 1961 and Hedtke was confined to a wheelchair but, well on her way to the century mark herself, she was full of life and anxious to exchange stories with her most famous pupil.

This is how long it had been: The mayor of Riverdale was Ed Kipley, Jr., the son of the man who grew up in the house behind Robinson's and worked out with her at Riverdale Park. A longtime employee of Acme Steel, Kipley Sr. had served as mayor himself from 1957 until 1967.

Thomas Kinney was another resident who wouldn't have missed the moment. He was the neighborhood youngster who recruited Betty for the talent show more than sixty years earlier, then helped park cars at the welcoming parade after her first Olympic victory. Kinney, 79, confessed he was among the boys who chased her on the playgrounds. "She'd beat all the guys," he said. "Nobody could catch her."[1]

They all had some catching up to do before and after they dedicated the park gazebo, which had been built expressly for that 1928 parade, to Betty. A commemorative plaque testifying to the occasion was affixed to a large rock in front of the structure on September 19. Billed as the feature event of the centennial picnic, it brought the recipient to tears.

Surrounded by her husband and son as well as nieces and nephews, she choked up as she tried to express her gratitude to her hometown. "I'll always be thankful I was born a runner," she said.[2]

Back in Colorado, where the Schwartzes moved to be closer to their daughter and three grandchildren, Betty again became a person of interest at the approach of the 1996 Olympics scheduled in Atlanta. Kodak, one of the official sponsors, offered a set of pins and photos featuring a star from Olympic Games on film cartons, with Betty representing the 1928 Olympics. Prior to releasing a card set of Olympic stars, including Robinson, the Upper Deck company invited Betty and her husband to a photo shoot in California, where they mingled with the likes of Muhammad Ali, Bob Mathias, Nadia Comaneci, and Florence Griffith-Joyner.

But the event that really engrossed Robinson was the torch relay, which had debuted at her final Olympics in Berlin and had grown into a major event in the ensuing years. In 1996 she was invited to carry the torch through a section of Denver on its way east to Georgia, and her life revolved around the endeavor in the days leading up to May 12.

Her memory was failing by then and, had somebody in charge asked her which city she was in on the day of the event, it's unlikely she would have answered correctly. But in the shuttle that dropped her off at her assigned spot, another torch bearer posed a question about 1928 and 84-year-old Betty Robinson Schwartz was transformed into the impressionable 16-year-old who delighted the fans in Amsterdam. She recalled every last detail and offered the story with the smiles and laugh lines all in place.

Still, she took her duty seriously that day. Accompanied by her daughter, Jane, and granddaughter, Brook, during her "run," she insisted on holding aloft the lit torch until passing on the flame to the next bearer. She offered a little cheer to the camera crew as it taped her moment and only surrendered the torch to a family member after the flame was extinguished. Betty was the oldest Olympic gold medalist to take part in the exercise and, likely, the proudest.

Dick Schwartz died the following year, and Rick flew west from Chicago to care for his mother, who made one last public appearance in June 1998. The occasion was the first Olympic Memorabilia and Coin Show, hosted by the U.S. Olympic Committee at its Colorado Springs headquarters.

The show featured coins, flags, pins, torches, and other prized souvenirs from Olympic Games dating back to the first modern Games in Athens.

"But, the greatest treasures there were not made of metal or cloth, they weren't kept behind a glass case away from the public's curious fingers, nor did they come from foreign lands," reported journalist

Julie Jagodzinske. "The most valuable mementos there were two of the U.S's most revered Olympians—Al Oerter and Betty Robinson Schwartz."[3]

Oerter, who was born one month after Robinson competed in Berlin, was the first track and field athlete to win an individual gold medal in four consecutive Olympic Games. Still, the discus king was no match for his elder when it came to interacting with fans. Focused as clearly as if she were still on the track, Robinson maintained a steady and witty dialogue while autographing "anything and everything" related to the Olympics, including photographs of her triumph in Amsterdam.

She also gained the advantage when the two were handed gold-plated scissors for the ribbon-cutting that symbolized the official opening of the event. Declining to wait for the signal from John Krimsky, the USOC deputy secretary general and managing director of business affairs, she made the first snip and the first boast.

"I'm still the fastest," she announced, to the amusement of the crowd.

It would be her final moment in the role she was born to play, the smiling champion. Diagnosed with cancer and with her mind clouded by the onset of Alzheimer's, she moved into her daughter's house and died on May 17, 1999.

"I never dreamed women's sports would become as big as it is," she noted in her later years as female basketball, soccer, and softball grew in popularity. "I think it's fantastic. When I started, women and even men in the middle classes didn't have the chance to compete or be discovered. I just happened to be one of the lucky ones, in the right place at the right time. . . . It's sad when you think about all the great competitors who remained unknown because they didn't have the opportunity."[4]

She declined to accept the mantle of crusader for women's rights. "I was too young to think about the first woman thing," Robinson said. "I was just thrilled to be there."[5]

Yet, in becoming the first of her sex to claim an Olympic gold medal in track and then overcoming a life-threatening accident to author one of the great comebacks in sports history, she served as a positive model for many.

Robinson's life story, according to the obituary written by Frank Litsky for the *New York Times*, "sounded like the product of an over-imaginative screenwriter."[6]

The fact that it was real, and not contrived, is cause for celebration.

## CHAPTER 20

# Legacy

One hundred years after her birth and a dozen years after her death, Betty Robinson remained a well of inspiration. Her story, while not nearly as familiar as that of other former Olympic champions, was retold during the run-up to the 2012 London Games.

In the care of Abigail Troshak, a student from York County School of Technology in Pennsylvania, it took the form of a class project that wound up on the desk of President Barack Obama and earned her a commendation from the chief executive. Robinson's story also was included on a motivational website that focused on successful athletes who had overcome extreme adversity to achieve their goals. And a magazine article listed her, in tongue-in-cheek fashion, first among "seven people whose death notices improved their lives."

All these developments transpired in 2011, a century after Robinson joined the human race in Riverdale, Illinois.

Troshak, who subsequently enrolled at Lycoming College, researched Robinson for a high school assignment on a figure in U.S. history and his or her impact. A track athlete herself, the girl suffered serious burns on her legs and feet in a kitchen fire in July 2009 and missed six months of school, yet returned not only to compete for the track team but to graduate with her peers.

"I was *the* track athlete at my school," Troshak said in a telephone interview, "a sprinter. I lost so much muscle mass in my legs that they didn't know if I was ever going to walk again, let alone run. But I pushed myself. Although I wasn't able to run as well as before, I could compete in the 4 × 400 relay and I started throwing the javelin, the shot put and the discus."

In Robinson, she found the perfect role model. "I saw her name on a list and I Googled it," Troshak said. "I had never even heard of her before but I was looking for a track athlete who had overcome traumatic injuries. There aren't any books on her. My library had absolutely nothing."

She eventually gleaned enough information to write an essay, which she presented before the class. Along with her classmates' projects, Troshak's essay was then sent to the president, who was invited to visit the school and listen to their presentations.

Unlike the efforts of classmates, many of whom focused on former presidents, Troshak's choice was personally motivated. "We both have gone through terrible physical pain and rehabilitation," Troshak explained, "yet we overcame those obstacles and followed our dreams."

Although Obama did not visit the school, he did send a reply that surprised and delighted the teenager. "I am inspired by the hope and determination of young people who have persevered in times of adversity to reach for their dreams," the president wrote back. "I admire your extraordinary courage and strength."[1]

A few months later, Robinson's story was revisited in a blog by Jeremy Holm, a bobsled pilot and motivational speaker who founded the Athlete Outreach Project. Placing her in the company of Olympic champions Wilma Rudolph, Jim Thorpe, Harold Connolly, Eric Liddell, and Kerri Strug—as well as professional athletes Jackie Robinson, George Foreman, and Jim Abbott—Holm used Betty's comeback to illustrate the power of a positive response.

"Life's 'Hard-Knocks 101' courses can be tough and come at less-than-desirable times," he wrote. "But we can all take a lesson from

Elizabeth 'Betty' Robinson. When the unexpected occurs, just keep running. Keep moving forward and don't give up. Take the time you need to heal and grow stronger from it. Don't quit. Don't become bitter. Dig deep and find the champion inside."[2]

The perception that Robinson had died after she was found in the twisted wreckage of her cousin's plane led the bimonthly magazine *Mental Floss* to consider her "Better Off Dead," along with the likes of Mark Twain, who testified that "reports of my death are greatly exaggerated," and Captain Eddie Rickenbacker, an American flying ace whose death was reported at least twice after air crashes—one at sea—that he survived.[3]

After reading her story in the magazine, Mike Smith wrote a blog for the website of Fluence, a dental practice marketing and management company, that extolled Robinson's virtues. "We all face setbacks and challenges," he wrote, "and at times our options may look much like Betty did on the mortician's table. However, most of us are only limited by how intensely we let the fire burn in our belly. We are all capable of much more than we imagine. If you want a pacesetter for what can be accomplished, I suggest Betty Robinson."[4]

For the Athlete Outreach Project, Holm also had a suggestion at the end of what he called a "life lesson" that starred "an athlete you've probably never heard of, but her story is one you'll never forget." Regarding Robinson, he said, "Some day someone is either going to write a book or make a movie about this incredibly inspiring woman!"[5]

Of course, the real legacy of Robinson, as well as the other eighteen pioneers who set foot aboard the SS *President Roosevelt* on that morning in July 1928, can be found in the access and opportunities for those who followed. Whereas they competed in only five events in Amsterdam, female track and field athletes had twenty-three contests from which to choose at the London Olympics.

Women represented only 14 percent of the American team that sailed for the Netherlands so long ago. Eighty-four years later, for the very first time, they constituted more than half of the athletes in the U.S. delegation at London. Of the forty-six gold medals earned by American individuals or teams, females accounted for twenty-nine, or 63 percent.

Robinson deserves a share of the credit. "Her role is the same even if people don't remember her," said Dr. Bill Mallon, a cofounder and past president of the International Society of Olympic Historians, in a 2012 telephone interview. "Young nurses today probably don't know [the story of] Florence Nightingale but it started with her."

A first lady, indeed.

# NOTES

### INTRODUCTION

1. "Women in the Olympic Games," *Olympic Review,* July 1912, 110–11.

2. Lissa Smith, ed., *Nike Is a Goddess: The History of Women in Sports* (New York: Atlantic Monthly Press, 1998), 6.

3. Ibid., 7.

4. Louise Mead Tricard, *American Women's Track and Field: A History, 1895 Through 1980* (Jefferson, N.C.: McFarland & Company), 188.

5. Mary H. Leigh and Therese M. Bonne, "The Pioneering Role of Madame Alice Milliat and the FSFI in Establishing International Track and Field Competition for Women," *Journal of Sport History* 4 (Spring 1977): 78.

6. Associated Press, May 2, 1928.

7. Susan K. Cahn, *Coming on Strong: Gender and Sexuality in Twentieth Century Women's Sports* (Cambridge, Mass., Harvard University Press, 1994), 63.

### CHAPTER 1

1. *New York Times,* May 21, 1999.

2. Doris H. Pieroth, *Their Day in the Sun: Women of the 1932 Olympics* (Seattle: University of Washington Press, 1996), 22.

3. Tricard, *American Women's Track and Field,* 139.

4. *Chicago Evening American,* May 29, 1928.

5. Ibid., June 4, 1928.

6. Thomas Kinney, letter to Riverdale Public Library, 1997.

7. Tricard, *American Women's Track and Field,* 124–25.

8. *Times-Standard,* Eureka, Calif., Dec. 1, 2001.

9. Tricard, *American Women's Track and Field,* 123.

### CHAPTER 2

1. Frederick Lewis Allen, *Only Yesterday: An Informal History of the 1920s* (New York: HarperCollins, 2010), 164, 193, 308.

2. *New York Times,* July 11–12, 1928.

3. Douglas MacArthur, *Reminiscences* (New York: McGraw-Hill, 1964), 82.

4. John A. Lucas, "USOC President Douglas MacArthur and His Olympic Moment, 1927–1928," *Olympika* 3 (1994): 112.

5. William Manchester, *American Caesar: Douglas MacArthur 1880–1964* (Boston: Little, Brown and Company, 1978), 137.

6. MacArthur, *Reminiscences,* 86.

7. Lewis H. Carlson and John J. Fogarty, *Tales of Gold* (Chicago: Contemporary Books, 1987), 92.

8. Manchester, *American Caesar,* 140.

9. Carlson and Fogarty, *Tales of Gold,* 92.

10. Ibid., 104.

11. Bud Greenspan, *America's Greatest Olympians.*

12. Tricard, *American Women's Track and Field,* 143.

13. Maybelle Reichardt Hopkins, *An Olympian's Oral History: Maybelle Reichardt Hopkins* (Amateur Athletic Foundation of Los Angeles), 10.

14. *Canyon Courier,* Evergreen, Col., Oct. 1988.

15. Tricard, *American Women's Track and Field,* 207.

16. Carlson and Fogarty, *Tales of Gold,* 139.

17. Jane Fauntz Manske, *An Olympian's Oral History: Jane Fauntz Manske* (Amateur Athletic Foundation of Los Angeles, 1988), 7.

18. Ernest "Nick" Carter, *An Olympian's Oral History: Ernest "Nick" Carter* (Amateur Athletic Foundation of Los Angeles, 1988), 21.

19. Manske, *An Olympian's Oral History,* 8.

20. Lucas, "USOC President Douglas MacArthur," 113.

21. Carlson and Fogarty, *Tales of Gold,* 53.

22. Manchester, *American Caesar,* 140.

CHAPTER 3

1. Associated Press, July 20, 1928.

2. Ibid.

3. Carter, *An Olympian's Oral History,* 25.

4. Anne Vrana O'Brien, *An Olympian's Oral History: Anne Vrana O'Brien* (Amateur Athletic Foundation of Los Angeles, 1988), 7.

5. *Glendale News-Press,* Glendale, Calif., Aug. 31, 1928.

6. Ibid.

7. Hopkins, *An Olympian's Oral History,* 10.

8. *Denver Post,* April 28, 1996.

9. Carlson and Fogarty, *Tales of Gold,* 54.

10. Ibid.

11. Carter, *An Olympian's Oral History,* 25.

12. *New York Times,* July 30, 1928.

13. Associated Press, July 30, 1928.

14. *New York Times,* July 31, 1928.

15. Louis Nixdorf, National Museum of American History, Archives Center.

16. Associated Press, July 30, 1928.

CHAPTER 4

1. *Chicago Evening American,* Aug. 24, 1928.

2. *New York Times,* Aug. 1, 1928.

3. Carlson and Fogarty, *Tales of Gold,* 80.
4. Associated Press, July 31, 1928.
5. *Chicago Evening American,* Aug. 1, 1928.
6. Carlson and Fogarty, *Tales of Gold,* 80–81.
7. Tricard, *American Women's Track and Field,* 139.
8. *Denver Post,* April 28, 1996.
9. MacArthur, *American Olympic Committee Report, Ninth Olympic Games,* 1.

CHAPTER 5
1. Tricard, *American Women's Track and Field,* 125.
2. *New York Times,* Aug. 2, 1928.
3. *New York Times,* Aug. 3, 1928.
4. Ibid.
5. Associated Press, Aug. 2, 1928.
6. Carter, *An Olympian's Oral History,* 28.
7. Carlson and Fogarty, *Tales of Gold,* 65.
8. Ibid.
9. Ibid., 65–66.
10. Associated Press, Aug. 3, 1928.
11. Carlson and Fogarty, *Tales of Gold,* 66.
12. *Denver Post,* April 28, 1996.
13. Douglas MacArthur, *American Olympic Committee Report,* 6.

CHAPTER 6
1. *Chicago Tribune,* Aug. 23, 1928.
2. Ibid.
3. *New York Times,* Aug. 23, 1928.
4. MacArthur, *American Olympic Committee Report,* 1.
5. *Chicago Evening American,* Aug. 23, 1928.
6. Ibid., Aug. 25, 1928.

CHAPTER 7
1. *Chicago Tribune,* Aug. 28, 1928.
2. *Chicago Evening American,* Aug. 28, 1928.
3. *Chicago Herald Examiner,* Aug. 28, 1928.
4. *Chicago Tribune,* Aug. 28, 1928.
5. Evelyne Hall Adams, *An Olympian's Oral History: Evelyne Hall Adams* (Amateur Athletic Foundation of Los Angeles, 1988), 6.
6. *Chicago Tribune,* Aug. 28, 1928.
7. Ibid.
8. *Chicago Evening American,* Aug. 29, 1928.
9. Kinney, Letter to Riverdale Public Library.

### CHAPTER 8

1. Anita DeFrantz, "The Changing Role of Women in the Olympic Games," *Olympic Review* 26, no. 15 (June–July 1997): 19.

2. *New York Times,* Aug. 3, 1928.

3. *The Times* (London), Aug. 3, 1928.

4. *Chicago Evening American,* Aug. 3, 1928.

5. Tricard, *American Women's Track and Field,* 175.

6. Stephanie Daniels and Anita Tedder, *A Proper Spectacle: Women Olympians 1900–1936* (London: ZeNaNa Press, 2000), 69.

7. O'Brien, *An Olympian's Oral History,* 9.

8. Francis-Marius Messerli, "Women's Participation in the Modern Olympic Games" (International Olympic Committee, 1952), 25–26.

9. Luke McKernan, "Rituals and ·Records: The Films of the 1924 and 1928 Olympic Games," *European Review* 19 (Aug. 30, 2011): 572.

10. *Chicago Evening American,* Aug. 25, 1928.

11. Tricard, *American Women's Track and Field,* 175.

12. Ibid., 176.

13. Allen Guttman, *The Games Must Go On: Avery Brundage and the Olympic Movement* (New York: Columbia University Press, 1983), 59.

14. *New York Times,* Sept. 9, 1960.

### CHAPTER 9

1. *Canyon Courier,* Oct. 1988.

2. Carlson and Fogarty, *Tales of Gold,* 83.

3. *Chicago Tribune,* Sept. 27, 1992.

4. Associated Press, July 27, 1929.

5. Tricard, *American Women's Track and Field,* 161.

6. *Chicago Tribune,* Oct. 17, 1930.

7. Ibid.

8. Ibid.

### CHAPTER 10

1. *Chicago Tribune,* June 29, 1931.

2. Carlson and Fogarty, *Tales of Gold,* 81.

3. *Chicago Evening American,* June 29, 1931.

4. Greenspan, *America's Greatest Olympians.*

5. *Chicago Tribune,* Aug. 5, 1931.

6. Carlson and Fogarty, *Tales of Gold,* 81.

7. *Chicago Tribune,* April 22, 1932.

8. Ibid., Dec. 22, 1931.

9. Ibid.

10. Tricard, *American Women's Track and Field,* 197.

11. David Wallechinsky, *The Complete Book of the Olympics* (Boston: Little, Brown and Company, 1992), 177.

12. Ibid., 143.

CHAPTER 11

1. Carlson and Fogarty, *Tales of Gold*, 81.

2. Sharon Kinney Hanson, *The Life of Helen Stephens: The Fulton Flash* (Carbondale: Southern Illinois University Press, 2004), 26.

3. *New York Times*, Sept. 15, 1935.

4. Tricard, *American Women's Track and Field*, 188.

5. Ibid., 231.

6. Ibid., 228.

7. *Denver Post*, April 28, 1996.

8. *New York Times*, July 5, 1936.

9. Carlson and Fogarty, *Tales of Gold*, 109.

10. *New York Times*, July 6, 1936.

11. Ibid.

12. Associated Press, July 9, 1936.

CHAPTER 12

1. David Clay Large, *Nazi Games: The Olympics of 1936* (New York: W. W. Norton & Company, 2007), 69–70.

2. Ibid., 79.

3. David Maraniss, *Rome 1960: The Olympics That Changed the World* (New York: Simon and Schuster, 2008), 67.

4. Large, *Nazi Games*, 90–91.

5. Ibid., 72.

6. Ibid., 84.

7. Ibid., 86.

8. Ibid., 87.

9. Guttman, *The Games Must Go On*, 74–75.

10. Large, *Nazi Games*, 91.

11. Ibid., 92.

12. John A. Lucas, "Judge Jeremiah T. Mahoney, the Amateur Athletic Union, and the Olympic Games," *Journal of Sport History* 35, no. 3 (Fall 2008): 504.

13. Ibid., 505.

14. Large, *Nazi Games*, 92.

15. Ibid., 93.

16. "The Movement to Boycott the Berlin Olympics of 1936," *Holocaust Encyclopedia* (Washington, D.C.: United States Holocaust Memorial Museum), 1–2.

17. Large, *Nazi Games*, 99.

18. Lucas, "Judge Jeremiah T. Mahoney," 505.

19. Large, *Nazi Games*, 100.

CHAPTER 13

1. Dr. James E. LuValle, *An Olympian's Oral History: Dr. James E. LuValle* (Amateur Athletic Foundation of Los Angeles, 1988), 9–10.

2. Hanson, *The Life of Helen Stephens*, 63.

3. United Press, July 15, 1936.

4. Ibid., July 17, 1936.

5. Ibid.

6. Iris Cummings Critchell, *An Olympian's Oral History: Iris Cummings Critchell* (Amateur Athletic Foundation of Los Angeles, 1988), 15.

7. Carlson and Fogarty, *Tales of Gold,* 150.

8. LuValle, *An Olympian's Oral History,* 16–17.

9. Carlson and Fogarty, *Tales of Gold,* 89.

10. Wallechinsky, *The Complete Book of the Olympics,* 532.

11. Hanson, *The Life of Helen Stephens,* 70.

12. Carlson and Fogarty, *Tales of Gold,* 90.

13. Ibid.

14. *New York Times,* July 25, 1936.

15. Joanna de Tuscan Harding, *An Olympian's Oral History: Joanna de Tuscan Harding* (Amateur Athletic Foundation of Los Angeles, 1988), 14.

16. Hanson, *The Life of Helen Stephens,* 73.


CHAPTER 14

1. Large, *Nazi Games,* 4–5.

2. Ibid., 192.

3. Malcolm W. Metcalf, *An Olympian's Oral History: Malcolm W. Metcalf* (Amateur Athletic Foundation of Los Angeles, 1988), 16.

4. *New York Times,* Aug. 2, 1936.

5. Ibid.

6. Ibid.

7. Ibid.

8. Ibid.

9. Ibid.

10. Ibid.


CHAPTER 15

1. Large, *Nazi Games,* 165.

2. Hanson, *The Life of Helen Stephens,* 87–88.

3. Carlson and Fogarty, *Tales of Gold,* 132.

4. Hanson, *The Life of Helen Stephens,* 90–91.


CHAPTER 16

1. Hanson, *The Life of Helen Stephens,* 98–99.

2. Ibid., 99.

3. Ibid.

4. Ibid., 101.

5. Large, *Nazi Games,* 240.

6. Associated Press, Aug. 4, 1936.

7. Large, *Nazi Games,* 241.

8. Ibid.

9. Associated Press, Aug. 7, 1936.

10. Large, *Nazi Games,* 241.

11. Avery Brundage, American Olympic Committee Report, 1936, Eleventh Olympic Games, 35.

12. Associated Press, Aug. 9, 1936.

13. Hanson, *The Life of Helen Stephens,* 103.

14. Carlson and Fogarty, *Tales of Gold,* 140.

15. German Organizing Committee, Official Report, 1936, Eleventh Olympic Games, 609.

16. *New York Times,* Aug. 10, 1936.

17. Carlson and Fogarty, *Tales of Gold,* 83.

18. Ibid., 140.

19. *New York Times,* Aug. 10, 1936.

20. Hanson, *The Life of Helen Stephens,* 104.

21. *New York Times,* Aug. 10, 1936.

22. Greenspan, *America's Greatest Olympians.*

23. *Chicago Tribune,* June 5, 1988.

24. Carlson and Fogarty, *Tales of Gold,* 83.

CHAPTER 17

1. Anthony Read, *The Devil's Disciples: Hitler's Inner Circle* (New York: W. W. Norton and Company, 2005), 421.

2. Critchell, *An Olympian's Oral History,* 28.

3. Carlson and Fogarty, *Tales of Gold,* 141.

4. Ibid., 141–42.

5. *Fort Myers News-Press,* Nov. 8, 1981.

6. *New York Times,* Aug. 29, 1936.

7. Ibid.

8. Ibid., Sept. 4, 1936.

9. *The Pointer* (Riverdale, Ill.), Sept. 4, 1936.

10. Ibid.

11. *New York Times,* Sept. 4, 1936.

12. Maraniss, *Rome 1960,* 68–69.

CHAPTER 18

1. Betty Robinson diary, private collection.

2. Ibid.

3. *Chicago Tribune,* Nov. 22, 1939.

4. George Beres, "Olympics Fist American Woman to Win a Gold Medal," *Omnibus,* November 1964, 43.

5. Wallechinsky, *The Complete Book of the Olympics,* 144.

6. USATF.org/haloffame/TF/Class of 1977.

7. *Denver Post,* April 28, 1996.

8. *Columbus Dispatch,* May 1, 1986.

CHAPTER 19

1. *Chicago Tribune,* Sept. 27, 1992.

2. Ibid.

3. Julie Jagodzinske, "Olympic Memorabilia and Coin Show," *The Olympian,* Summer 1998, 6.

4. *Fort Myers News-Press,* Nov. 8, 1981.

5. *USA Today,* Jan. 18, 1984.

6. *New York Times,* May 21, 1999.

CHAPTER 20

1. *York Daily Record/Sunday News,* June 27, 2011.

2. Athleteoutreach.com/index.php/Elizabeth-robinson-plane-crash-survivor-gold-medalist.

3. *Mental Floss* 10, no. 4 (July–August 2011).

4. Fluenceportland.com/strategy/back-from-the-dead-to-win-the-gold, July 12, 2011.

5. Athleteoutreach.com.

# INDEX

Abbott, Jim, 174
Abrahams, Harold, 71
Abramson, Jesse, 96
Albritton, Dave, 165–66
Albus, Emmy, 135, 136, 144–46
Alderman, Fred, 53
Ali, Muhammad, 169
Allen, Frederick Lewis, 19–20
Amateur Athletic Union (AAU), 5, 10, 14, 16, 74–75, 88–89, 99, 112
American Olympic Committee (AOC), 7, 20, 59, 75, 102–4, 106, 112–13, 115, 120
Anderson, Stephen, 48
Atkinson, Sydney, 48

Baillet-Latour, Henri, 55, 75, 107, 109–10, 111–12, 122, 126–27, 135, 151, 161
Baird, George, 53
Ball, James, 51, 53
Ball, Rudi, 108
Barbuti, Ray, 50–53, 54, 55, 58–60
Beamon, Bob, 163
Bell, Jane, 40
Bergmann, Gretel, 108, 117
Bingham, Bill, 103
Birchall, Frederick T., 127, 128, 131
Bland, Harriet, 97, 100, 101, 103, 135, 139, 142, 144, 150, 152, 155, 165
Boeckmann, Delores (Dee), 23–24, 90, 97–98, 163; and 1936 Olympics, 102, 103, 116, 117, 121, 137–42, 145, 152
Borah, Charlie, 48, 53
Bracey, Claude, 36
Bremen, Wilhelmina von, 92–93

Brix, Herman, 35
Brundage, Avery, 75, 79, 99, 103, 106–7, 110–14, 116–17, 119, 121–22, 139, 144, 156–57

Carew, Mary, 92
Carr, Sabin, 49
Carter, Nick, 26, 34, 50–51
Cartwright, Elta, 15–16, 37, 48, 90
Catherwood, Ethel, 40, 53
Cecil, David George Brownlow, Lord Burghley, 35–36
Chicago Evening American, 11–13, 14, 17–18, 44–45, 60, 65–67, 77, 87
Coachman, Alice, 163
Collier, John, 48
Comaneci, Nadia, 169
Connolly, Harold, 174
Considine, Bob, 59
Cook, Myrtle, 37, 39–40, 41–42, 44, 53–54, 81, 83
Coolidge, Calvin, 55, 59
Copeland, Lillian, 40, 90, 92
Corcoran, Jimmy, 12, 60–62, 65–67
Coubertin, Pierre de, 3–4, 5–6, 30, 79
Crabbe, Buster, 25
Cromwell, Dean, 144
Cross, Jessie, 15–16, 47–48, 80, 90
Cuhel, Frank, 35
Cummings, Iris, 117–18, 150

Daley, Arthur, 76, 146
Day, Leighton, 48
DeFrantz, Anita, 69
Dempsey, Jack, 153, 154
Denis, Henri, 34
Desjardins, Pete, 55

Didrikson, Mildred (Babe), 81,
  88–89, 91–92, 98–99, 134, 147, 163
Diem, Carl, 107, 126, 131
Dollinger, Marie, 135, 136, 144–47
Dorffeldt, Ilse, 144–47, 151
Draper, Foy, 143–44, 145

Earhart, Amelia, 3, 20, 63
Ederle, Gertrude, 154
Egg, Eleanor, 88
El Ouafi, Boughera, 53

Faggs, Mae, 163
"Fair Play for American Athletes,"
  111
Fauntz, Jane, 25–26
Fédération des Sociétés Féminines
  Sportives de France, 4
Fédération Sportive Féminine Inter-
  nationale (FSFI), 5–6, 12
Femina Sport, 4
Ferris, Daniel F., 98, 102
Filkey, Helen, 10, 12, 14–16, 44–45,
  78, 80, 88–89
Fleischer, Tilly, 134
Foreman, George, 174
Furtsch, Evelyn, 92

Garland, William May, 107, 112, 113
Geiger, Edward J., 45
Germany, 1936 Games controversy,
  105–14, 122–24, 156–57
Gilman, Marion, 23
Glickman, Marty, 143–44, 145
Goebbels, Joseph, 125–26, 131, 139,
  149
Göring, Hermann, 126, 139, 149–50
Gould, Alan, 121
Graham, Otto, 165
Green, Theodore, 100
Griffith-Joyner, Florence, 169
Grobes, Elizabeth, 16

Hahn, Lloyd, 48–49
Hall, Evelyne, 83–84, 92

Halt, Karl Ritter von, 106
Hardin, Glenn, 136
Harrington, Ethel, 84, 101
Hasenfus, Olive, 6, 15, 16–17, 23, 90,
  101, 116, 151
Hayhurst, Norm, 31–32
Hedtke, Florence, 167–68
Hein, Karl, 135
Helms Athletic Foundation, 163
Hendrik, 31, 32–33, 34, 55
Herron, Laura, 16
Herschfeld, Emil, 35
Hess, Rudolf, 137–39
Hill, Frank, 82, 84, 88, 89, 165
Hiscock, Eileen, 135
Hitler, Adolf, 102, 105–6, 108,
  123–29, 133–38, 144, 147, 156,
  165–66
Hitomi, Kinue, 37, 70, 72
Holley, Marion, 90
Holm, Eleanor, 23, 119–22, 139, 152
Holm, Herbert, 121
Holm, Jeremy, 174–75
Houser, Bud, 7, 27, 33, 49
Hulbert, Murray, 75

Illinois Catholic Women's Club,
  100–101, 156
Illinois State Athletic Association, 9
Illinois Women's Athletic Club
  (IWAC), 10–11, 14, 25, 64, 66, 78,
  83–84, 85, 91, 95–96, 100
International Amateur Athletic Fed-
  eration (IAAF), 5, 74–75
International Ladies Games, 5
International Olympic Committee
  (IOC), 4–6, 30, 55, 69, 73–74, 75,
  105, 107, 110, 113, 126, 164
Ismayr, Rudolf, 130

Jagodzinske, Julie, 170
Jahncke, Ernest, 107, 109–10,
  113–14
Jarrett, Eleanor Holm. See Holm,
  Eleanor

Jenkins, Margaret, 16, 40, 90, 92
Johnson, Cornelius, 134

Kanopacka, Halina, 40
Kelly, Edward J., 154–55, 156
Kelly, Kathlyn, 103, 116–18, 139
King, Robert, 35
Kinney, Thomas, 13–14, 67, 168
Kinney Hanson, Sharon, 121,
    136–39, 142, 145, 147
Kipley, Ed, 79, 168
Kirby, Gustavus T., 74, 75, 104, 107
Koernig, Helmut, 48, 54
Krauss, Käthe, 96, 135, 136, 144–46
Kuck, John, 34–35

Ladoumègue, Jules, 48
La Guardia, Fiorello, 154
Lammers, Georg, 36
Lanzi, Mario, 136
Large, David Clay, 105–6, 108–9,
    110–11, 113, 125–26, 133–34,
    143–44
Larva, Harri, 48
Lasker, Albert, 113
Lawson, J. Hubert, 120
Legg, Wilfred, 36
Lewald, Theodor, 110–11, 127, 129
Liddell, Eric, 174
Lincoln Park Athletic Association,
    96, 100
Lindbergh, Charles, 64, 127
Litsky, Frank, 171
London, Jack, 36
Long, Luz, 136
Louis, Spyridon, 130
Lucas, John A., 110, 112
LuValle, Jim, 115, 119

MacArthur, Douglas, 3, 7, 21–23,
    26–27, 29, 33, 35, 45–46, 51–53,
    54–55, 59–61, 79, 116, 163
MacDonald, Rena, 40, 70, 80, 90
Maguire, Catherine, 23–24, 90
Mahoney, Jeremiah T., 110–11, 112

Mallon, Bill, 176
Manchester, William, 22
Maranis, David, 106–7, 156
Mathias, Bob, 169
Mauermayer, Gisela, 136
Mayer, Helene, 108–9, 117
McAllister, Bob, 36
McDonald, Florence, 70, 90
McElroy, Kathleen, 5
McGrath, Matt, 59, 154
McKean, Olive, 120
McKernan, Luke, 72
McNeil, Loretta, 15, 16, 47–48, 80,
    90
Messerli, Franz M., 72, 73
Metcalf, Malcolm, 127
Metcalfe, Ralph, 83, 135, 143–44,
    145
Milliat, Alice, 4–5
Millrose Athletic Association, 15,
    47, 80
Minke, Jacob, 87
Moore, Bert, 97–99

Napolilli, Eddie, 160
National Women's Track and Field
    Committee, 4
Nixdorff, Louis, 37
Northern California Athletic Club,
    14–15, 47
Nurmi, Paavo, 35, 48

Obama, Barack, 174, 175
O'Brien, Anne Vrana. See Vrana,
    Anne
O'Callaghan, Patrick, 36
Oerter, Al, 170
Olympic Games: 1908 (London),
    33, 47; 1912 (Stockholm), 4, 23,
    47, 48, 59, 106; 1920 (Antwerp),
    5, 30; 1924 (Paris), 5, 24, 27, 30,
    54, 71; 1928 (Amsterdam), 3, 5,
    6, 23, 25, 27–37, 39–55, 69–76,
    90, 108, 133–34, 168, 169, 175;
    1932 (Los Angeles), 23, 25, 74–75,

88, 90, 91–93, 108, 111, 134, 144;
1936 (Berlin), 23, 102–3, 121,
125–31, 133–51; 1948 (London),
75; 1960 (Rome), 76, 163; 1996
(Atlanta), 168–69; 2012 (London),
173, 175–76; founding of modern
games, 3–4, 169
Owens, Jesse, 104, 134–35, 136, 139,
143–44, 145, 153, 155, 165–66

Paddock, Charley, 7, 31, 48
Palmer, Wilson, 85–86, 87
Pasadena Athletic Club, 15, 16
Pegler, Westbrook, 57
Petty, Mary Lou, 120
Phillips, Herman, 52
Pickett, Tidye, 92, 99, 103, 116, 118,
142, 152
Pierson, Bessie Bragg, 64
Pius XI, 6
Poynton, Dorothy, 23, 152–53
Price, Charles, 9–10, 68, 78, 82, 167
Prout, William, 5, 21

Quinn, Jimmy, 53

Radke, Lina, 70, 134
Rangely, Walter, 48
Ray, Joie, 53
Read, Anthony, 149
Reich, Bill, 66, 67–68
Reichardt, Maybelle, 24, 32, 40, 90
Riefenstahl, Leni, 139
Riel, Bert, 82–83, 88, 89, 95
Ritola, Willie, 35
Robertson, Lawson, 29, 143, 145
Robinson, Betty: 1928 Olympics, 3, 6,
37, 39–47, 53–55, 101, 148; 1932
Olympics, 79; 1936 Olympics, 103,
139, 141–42, 144–48, 151; appear-
ance, 81; "Artemis" nickname, 46,
60, 163; college activities, 82–84,
89, 165; early years, 7, 13–14, 168;
family, 13, 57, 61–62, 68, 86, 87–88,
89, 95–96, 154, 161; final years,

167–71; Great Depression years,
95–96; marriages, 159–61; plane
crash and recovery, 85–88, 89–90,
95, 175; post-crash comeback, 96–
97, 99–101, 170–71; post-Olympics
career, 161–63; pre-Olympics career, 9–18; quoted, 9–10, 11, 12, 17,
25, 32, 40–41, 42, 43–44, 54, 62, 64,
73, 82, 87–88, 89–90, 95, 101, 148,
159–60, 162, 164, 165, 168, 170;
return from 1928 Olympics, 57–68;
return from 1936 Olympics, 152–
57; senior year high school, 77–80;
television appearance, 163; track
meets: American Institute of Banking, 10; Central AAU, 11–13, 18,
83–84, 90, 97, 99; Illinois National
Guard and Militia, 83; Milwaukee,
84; national AAU championships,
80, 81, 83, 90–91, 100–101; Newark
Velodrome, 15–18, 47; trip to 1928
Olympics, 20–24; trip to 1936
Olympics, 116–17, 121–23
Robinson, Bill, 154, 155
Robinson, Jackie, 174
Robinson, Roger, 72–73
Rochfort, Jim, 89
Rockne, Knute, 43, 70–71
Rogers, Annette, 92, 99–101, 103,
116, 135–36, 141, 144, 147–48,
155–56, 165
Roosevelt, Franklin D., 112
Rosenfeld, Fanny, 37, 39–40, 42–43, 53
Rubien, Frederick W., 98
Rudolph, Wilma, 163, 174
Russell, Gloria, 80
Russell, Henry, 36, 53, 54
Ruth, Babe, 61–62, 53

Sachs, Beatrice, 64
Sackett, Ada Taylor, 120–21
Sayer, Edna, 15, 16, 90
Schaller, Simone, 116
Schilgen, Fritz, 130
Schmeling, Max, 139

Schmidt, Leni, 41–42
Scholz, Jackson, 48, 163
Schwartz, Richard, 159–61, 163, 169
Sentman, Lee, 83
Sheppard, Mel, 47–48, 80, 154
Sherrill, Charles, 107–9, 117
Shiley, Jean, 17, 23, 25, 90–92, 101–2
Shirer, William, 42–43
Smith, Al, 60, 107, 153
Smith, Ethel, 40, 42–43
Smith, Helen, 74–75
Smith, Mike, 175
Spencer, Bud, 51, 53
Steers, Fred, 65, 155
Steinberg, Erna, 42
Stephens, Helen, 97–102, 103,
   116–17, 121, 123, 135–39, 141–42,
   144–48, 150–53, 155, 163, 164–65
Stephens, Joseph, 78
Stewart, Harry Eaton, 4, 5, 73
Stokes, Louise, 92, 116, 118
Stoller, Sam, 143–44, 145
Strauss, Richard, 130, 139
Strike, Hilde, 93
Strug, Kerri, 174

Taylor, Morgan, 35–36
Terwilliger, Mary, 101
Thompson, Jean, 40
Thorpe, Jim, 174
Tobin, Edward J., 67
Todd, Nellie, 14, 15, 16
Torrance, Jack, 119, 134
Tricard, Louise Mead, 81
Troshak, Abigail, 173–74
Tschammer und Osten, Hans von, 108
Tunis, John R., 71, 75
Tuscan, Joanna de, 122–23

USA Track and Field Hall of Fame,
   163, 164

Venzke, Gene, 152
Vrana, Anne, 15–17, 23, 31, 37, 48,
   71, 90, 102, 103, 116

Walasiewicz, Stanisława. See Walsh,
   Stella
Walker, James J., 58–59
Wallechinsky, David, 91–93, 119–20,
   164
Walsh, Stella, 80–82, 83, 85, 88,
   92–93, 96–98, 99–100, 135–36,
   151, 163–64
Warren, Josephine, 101
Washburn, Mary, 15, 16, 37, 47–48, 80
Waterman, Elizabeth, 14
Weissmuller, Johnny, 7, 24, 25–26,
   27, 33, 55
Wever, Elfriede, 72
Whalen, Grover Aloysius, 19–20,
   47, 153
Widermann, Jane, 64
Wiley, Mildred, 6, 53, 90
Wilhelmina, 31, 32, 55
Williams, Archie, 118–19
Williams, Bob, 10
Williams, Percy, 36, 48
Williams, Wythe, 36–37, 41–42,
   54–55, 70
Wils, Jan, 31
Wilson, Rayma, 16, 90
Wittmann, Gundel, 43
Wollke, Hans, 134
women and sports, attitudes toward,
   4–6, 14, 70–75, 78, 161, 162, 170
women in the Olympics: displays
   of "feminine" behavior, 41–42,
   70–72, 76; resistance to, 3–6,
   69–76, 99
Women's Olympic Games (1922), 5
Women's World Championships
   (1930), 81–82
Woodruff, John, 136
Worst, Martha, 102
Wright, Margaret, 98
Wykoff, Frank, 31, 36, 53, 143–44,
   145, 163

Zamperini, Lou, 119